ROUI IRELAND WITH (AND WITHOUT) A HORSE

STEPHEN A CAWLEY

Joe Mackle
owns this book.

S☀CCIONES

ISBN: 9781790161997

Cover design & formatting by Socciones Editoria Digitale
www.socciones.co.uk

For Paul 'the bull' McCabe.
A man of courage vision and integrity.
Proud to call him my friend.

Never forgetting my mum.

Cawley and McCabe have winners. The Curragh July 2017.

CONTENTS

ACKNOWLEDGEMENTS

The vast majority of this book is based on my own travels and findings when following the horses in Ireland. However I am indebted to and acknowledge below some book and web sources that proved useful along the way.

An Arm and Four Legs, Stan Hey, Yellow Jersey Press, 1998

Top 100 Racehorses Of All Time, Robin Oakley, Corinthian Books, 2012

Horses For Courses, Anne Holland, Mainstream, 2005

Irish Horse-racing An Illustrated History, John Welcome, Macmillan, 1982

Mr Darley's Arabian, Christopher McGrath, John Murray, 2016

Racingpost.com

www.hri (Horse Racing Ireland)

I would also like to take the opportunity to thank my beautiful and talented wife Sue, my defacto editor and who became paparazzi as we followed the horses around Ireland.

Thanks to my brother, Ray, for his help with the family tree.

PREFACE

Horse racing may well be the sport of Kings, but my previous horse 'owning' experiences had taught me, that there was plenty of room for the common man! Both in **"Four Hooves and a Prayer"** and **"I Really Gotta Horse"**, I had managed to gain various forms of 'ownership' on a bare minimum in terms of financial outlay. These 'shoestring' methods had enabled me to enter the owners' ring with 'my' horses at some very prestigious horse race meetings. In so doing I gained something of an insider's view into the arcane world of racehorse ownership.

Buoyed with my success and while researching the family history of my parents' birthplace in Ireland, I suddenly thought of a wonderful idea: why not have a horse that would race in the Emerald Isle?

Surely, isn't Ireland the land of the horse? Where better to see if my 'shoestring' methods could work once more, and perhaps take me to some of the country's premier racecourses, or maybe even out west, where my ancestors came from.

While there is little doubt that to achieve this objective plentiful supplies of money are usually required, the 'shoestring' ownership model used in my previous adventures showed what could be possible. Fully aware of Flann O' Brien's immortal dictum; 'When money's tight and is hard to get and your horse has also ran', I felt I had the requisite experience to bring this particular dream about.

I am proud to say that I am a born and bred Mancunian, but I am equally proud of my Irish roots. I had been back to the country on countless occasions, never bothering to formalise such travel arrangements with an Irish passport, surely that would be somewhat ostentatious? However, by 2017 I was one of thousands of people who had now obtained an Irish passport, I am not certain what brought about this surge in numbers, I think it was to do with something that had happened in 2016! Whatever, it gave my search for an 'Irish racehorse', a certain authenticity.

The essence of my adventures that are outlined on the following pages was to see if I could manage the trick of having some horses that would run at Irish racecourses over a fourteen-month period between 2017 and 2018. It could be that your horse might simply be making up the numbers, Flan O'Brien's 'also ran', it could even be a potential winner or it might not get to the races at all. When you are operating from the other side of the Irish Sea on a limited budget, then this last scenario made for a very precarious state of affairs.

For the uninitiated, there is a world of difference between a horse being entered for a race and one that is declared to run. The entry stage is usually about a week before a race, if a trainer enters a horse then this would alert me to the fact that the horse may run in this race. May is the operative word as there are a multitude of reasons why the horse may not run! It could be the going will change and suddenly become unfavourable for 'our' horse, the competition may look too strong, the weight the horse is allocated to carry may be too much, the horse may be off colour or quite simply your trainer will opt to go elsewhere. The declaration stage is usually twenty four to forty eight hours before the race, if your horse reaches this point, you can then begin to have serious thoughts that your horse will indeed participate in the race. Even then it is possible that your horse may still not turn up for this race, and I have known of horses withdrawn from a race just before the start!

Given my distance across the Irish sea and the 'shoestring' budget allocated, one can see how hazardous it was for me to actually get 'my'; horse to the races! One didn't want to be haring over the Irish Sea to all points west; only to find when you got there that your horse was a non-starter. To some extent it was inevitable that there would be occasions when the horse may not run, but generally I had to be able to move as soon as I got some definite news about a race meeting that I could make. It was obvious from the outset that I would need a great deal of luck if I was to see some horses run back in the 'old country', but in a way such unpredictability was part of the adventure.

This book tells the story of my attempts to see 'my' horses run in Ireland. The horse racing element of the book will follow the template laid down in the earlier two books in this series, in that there will be an outline of the horse involved in the race, a description of the racecourse and then an account of the horse racing activity. Given the nature of this odyssey, it seems appropriate to outline the various places that I stopped at on the way. Ireland is a beautiful country; the gorgeous green landscape made up of mountains and beaches is worth a visit even without a horse! Therefore each chapter will also include a section on accommodation, where to obtain the best Guinness and areas of historical interest, all obviously available to those on a 'shoestring' budget!

Given that this story started with my research into a family line I traced back to Mayo in the mid 19th Century, it seemed appropriate to revisit those locations where my people hailed from. Given that I was visiting a country famed for its historic racing achievements, I was hoping that my visits would coincide with one of 'my' horses running way out west. Could I bring the dream about? In horse racing, as in life nothing is certain, but surely it was going to be good fun finding out.

Steve Cawley. Manchester. October. 2018.

The author hard at work researching the shoestring project! Navan, September 2017.

1

ROOTS

I had discovered, through my previous horse owning activities, just what an important factor breeding was in the world of horse racing. Whenever, a syndicate got in touch with a prospective horse, great store was placed on that horse's breeding pedigree. If it could be proved that the bloodline of the horse was an impressive one, then this could be seen as favourable for the horse's future prospects and therefore attractive to potential investors. In **"Four Hooves and a Prayer"**, I had attempted to encapsulate what this meant when I talked about it being a mix of the qualities inherited from the horse's dam (mother) and sire (father). In simple terms if the dam had won distance races and had already produced horses that were winning prestigious races and the sire had been a top class sprinter, that now commanded a hefty fee for his services at stud, then any progeny (offspring) from these two horses, potentially could be top class.

Of course in human terms, this concept of breeding was fundamental in producing the blue bloods that had ruled the country for many centuries past. Instead of stamina and speed, the prerequisites were family, wealth and status and inter marriage kept the elite at their proper station.

Myself, coming from parents born into relative poverty in the west of Ireland at the outset of the twentieth century, I was never likely to lead a life of privilege associated with the blue bloods. My increasing interest in horses combined with the momentous decision in the UK of June 26, 2016, suddenly had me searching my own family roots, in order to obtain an Irish passport. Procuring all the relevant documentation was a tortuous process and it broadened my understanding of my own family background.

My parents were born at the start of the second decade of the twentieth century, they were children of troubled times in Ireland of the Easter rising, the war of independence with the British and the Irish civil war. The impact of this on me a century later, was that it created a lot of difficulties in obtaining the genuine certificates required to obtain the increasingly popular Irish passport. In particular the Customs house fire of 1921 (at the peak of the war) appeared to have obliterated all the birth certificates of my parents, a problem that took me quite some time to resolve. The convoluted path of attempting to get hold of these essential documents took me on a journey back into my family roots that led from the west of Ireland in the nineteenth century to twentieth century Manchester.

When there is a lack of hard evidence regarding family history, all sorts of romantic notions can come to mind. In terms of Irish descent, there is the very broad distinction between the 'black' and 'red' line of family heritage. With my former black hair, brown eyes and some would say dark countenance; I came from the 'black line'. One theory is that the 'black Irish' were descendents of the Spanish Armada. Philip the second of Spain's attempted invasion of England in 1588 failed and blown off course and in disarray some of the ships came to grief on the rocks off the west coast of Ireland. I had many times been on the scenic and dramatic Atlantic drive along the coast at Achill which features the concrete viewing point that records the event. The swarthy dark Spaniards that managed to avoid being butchered by the locals, eventually settled in this part of the World. Who knows maybe my physical appearance can be linked to these people. Such thoughts though must remain supposition, as it proved virtually impossible to find any documentation for my family before the mid nineteenth century.

A couple of centuries before that, Oliver Cromwell had left his imprint on the 'west'. Old Ironsides, was no friend of Erin, indeed his name is associated with conquest and the brutal suppression of the local inhabitants. Commonwealth soldiers and adventurers who had supported Cromwell were rewarded with some of the best land in Ireland, the dispossessed were of course bound for 'hell or Connacht'. The land out west would have been some of the poorest and remotest in the whole island and I suppose for those relatives I could only speculate about, it would have made for a tough existence. Cromwell remained a bogyman for many out west, when I was born in Manchester over three hundred years later, my mother's inexplicable first choice of name apparently was, Oliver.

I had my elder sisters to thank for dissuading her from that choice, as they pointed out the association with the Lord Protector. My mother's explanation was that she was in fact naming me after the revered martyr Oliver Plunket; luckily my sisters won the argument.

The furthest back I could reach in terms of my documented family history was in the 1850s with the birth of Anthony Carey, my grandfather on my mother's side. Strictly speaking I had also unearthed his parents' details, so my great grandfather was called Hugh (1820-95) and he had been married to Mary Flannery (1816-1902), and they had resided in Bangor Erris, County Mayo. My grandfather had been born in 1855, just after the Great Famine (1845-49) had decimated the Country, with over a million dead and another million forced to migrate. The killer fungus, phytophthora infestans, started to destroy the potato crop, this was particularly bad in impoverished Mayo, where it was estimated that 90 percent of the population were dependent on the staple crop. The Irish population was instantly cut from eight million to six and over the next hundred years it continued to decline, in demographic terms, a freak amongst European Nations. For my great grandparents and Anthony Carey, mere survival must have been a singular achievement against such a backdrop of poverty and blight.

For Anthony Carey the land may have been poor, but Gladstone's enlightened land acts of the late 19th Century, meant that it would become possible for him to own that most precious of commodities in a rural environment; the 'land'. Anthony Carey would have had a 'ladder' farm that became common in the west, usually strips of land that would cut across good and poor land, with field boundaries, the rungs of that ladder.

The 'land' poor or not, was presumably enough capital on which to base a 'match' or marriage to my grandmother, Bridget Carey (no relation) in 1902. She was twenty-six at the time, and their union brought about eight children, before Anthony died in 1920. My mother Bridget (1912-95) was the sixth child born and she had five sisters and two brothers. Almost from birth their futures would be determined by poverty and lack of opportunity. The eldest child Mary (1903-93) married and stayed in the west all her life. The second son Hugh (1909-90) inherited the farm at Bangor Erris and also stayed all his life in the old country.

The other son John (1905-1978) settled in eastern England. The youngest child Sarah (1918-2009) also married and stayed next to the original farmstead. All the others including my mother eventually migrated to England, concentrating in the North West and Greater Manchester in particular. Katie (1906-99) and Sheila (1914-76) settled in south Manchester near my mother, whereas Eileen (1916-2010) settled near Wigan and actually returned to the west in 1994.

On my father's side of the family (the Cawleys) a similar story was to be traced. My grandfather William was born at Ardagh in Mayo in 1871. He actually migrated to England as a young man, settling in Leeds in 1899. He lived in the northern city for nine years only returning to the west in 1908 for the classic rural tradition of buying into a 'match'. Outside of Manchester, Leeds was to prove something of a recurrent theme, with my Father living there in the 1930s, my sister Maura settled there in the 1960s and I myself lived there as a student in the 1970s. Whilst in Leeds William had saved money from regular employment, it was this capital that allowed him to make a 'match', with my grandmother, Mary Walsh. Mary had been born in Barnfield in 1888 to a carpenter, my great grandfather, Tommy Walsh. In the local economy, it would seem that Tommy was a man of some moderate means and therefore in possession of 'land'. Once more the Gladstone legislation had enabled Tommy to own thirty acres of land, located alongside the railway that ran from the nearby township of Balina to Dublin. Unfortunately Tommy had died of burns in an accident in 1908 and Mary as the eldest child had inherited the land. William Cawley with his capital from Leeds bought into the 'match' and by marrying Mary Walsh in 1909, in effect took on the thirty acres of land to be farmed at Barnfield.

As with the Careys a number of children quickly resulted from this union. Patrick (1910-1988) was quickly followed by my father Martin (December 1910-2000), and a daughter Evelyn (1912-1978), who eventually took the other migrant route, emigrating to America where she married a retired New York policeman, returning in 1953 and buying land that adjoined the Cawley family plot. These elder three were joined by; Bertha (1916-2000), William (1920-1977), Thomas (1926-2018) and Michael (1926-2004). Michael's birth most unfortunately marked the death of Mary, who died in childbirth. In a rural society of that time, so many births in a short period of time was not unusual, in an age before birth control, having a lot of children was a norm established because of the high rate of infant mortality. Unfortunately maternal mortality was similarly an ever-present danger.

All the brothers with the exception of Tommy emigrated to England. My father did this in two separate phases. The story goes that as a nineteen year old he was sent off on some menial errand to collect animal feedstuffs in Balina, but instead he jumped on the Dublin train and ended up doing seasonal agricultural work in Lincolnshire. This story always surprised me it was hard to imagine the extremely cautious man of later life being such a spontaneous migrant, the impetuosity of youth no doubt. It was a short-term move, as he returned to Ireland in 1930 and stayed on the farm until 1935. However, with the worst effects of the depression receding he returned to England on a permanent basis from the mid thirties onwards, finding work and settling in Leeds and later Warrington and Manchester.

My mother followed the classic migrant pattern of connecting up with an extended family member as she moved to Manchester as a twenty year old. She moved in with her elder sister Mary's sister in law, living in inner city Ancoats, part of Manchester's little Ireland district. She worked in domestic service and eventually followed one of the affluent ladies she worked for to the posh seaside resort of Southport, where she resided for some years. By 1941 domestic service brought her back to south Manchester where she entered into employment for a Greek lady who would become a life long acquaintance. Living on Palatine Road (known locally as Palestine Road, due to the high proportion of wealthy foreign residents), she was in effect settling in the locality that would become her home for the rest of her life. It was from here in the second year of the Second World War that she married Martin Cawley. Two years later they moved into the house that would be home to myself, and my siblings, Northern Grove, West Didsbury.

In theory when William Cawley died in 1950, my father as the second eldest could have had a claim on the land and if he had gone back, I may have been born in Ireland five years later! However this was not part of the family equation and Tom the youngest who had stayed working the land inherited the farm. Over the next half century he farmed the 'land' even absorbing his sister Evelyn's land on her death in the seventies. As the Celtic tiger boomed in the early years of the twenty first century he was even able to sell off some strips of land for the construction of houses. He ended up a farmer of pedigree sheep, being the last of the siblings of either family and he died at the grand old age of ninety-four in 2018. The 'land' so vital a commodity at the time of the match in 1909, had proved to be a very valuable asset. Given the traditional picture of struggle for farmers on the land out west it may not be fanciful to suggest that the capital asset he owned at the time of his death was worth a good deal of money. This was somewhat ironic as all his brothers had followed the traditional migrant pattern of seeking out a better life elsewhere, but all probably never achieved Tom's financial status.

In their different ways both my mother and father adjusted well to their life in England, and when I arrived in 1955, I was brought up in a Mancunian household. I had joined an existing family of Raymond (1942), Maura (1944) and Elaine (1947); Catherine would join us in 1958. Influences of the old Country persisted not least in terms of religious observation and educational aspiration, but we weren't off to a ceilidh every weekend, we were Mancunians who enjoyed a two-week family holiday back in the west, every couple of years. To some degree children of Irish migrants are in the classic dilemma of being theoretical outsiders. In England they could be outsiders because of accent, cultural habits or religious observation. In Ireland, the accents and cultural habits picked up in England could similarly mark them as different to the indigenous population; 'Irish blood English heart', as Morrissey might put it.

My mother despite a deep-rooted love of the 'old' country understood where we were at and helped in our natural assimilation in the country of our birth. I was nicknamed 'Pom' by my brother and fitted in naturally to the anglicised influences that my mother was bringing into the house via her domestic service experience. Whether it was the hand me down clothing I received from the rich children of my mother's employers' or the more subtle influences that led to a life long support of the Manchester Guardian and radio four. However the Mayo of her youth was never forgotten and she was always the prime instigator of summer holidays back to Ireland. I never saw much in the way of horses on the land back in Mayo, I had to settle for the donkeys that pulled the turf down the old bog road. The nearest I came to any racehorses was when my cousin Mickey was looking after two 'resting' horses, but I deemed them too far off in the top fields to merit a visit! That all changed in 2017 when having found out so much about my family roots I decided that I would extend the racehorse ownership on a shoestring model to incorporate 'owning' a racehorse or two who would race back in the 'old country'.

The author at the graveside of his Grandparents. Mayo August 2018.

2

THE CURRAGH

When it comes to breeding the Elite racing club has a lot to be proud of. Although a cheap as chips racing club (based in England) they have over the years, boxed well above their weight by producing their own racehorses, some of which went to the very top of their discipline. The Club is a perfect example of how from time to time it is possible to produce a flat horse that can race on level terms with the sport's blue bloods, which are expensively purchased by the Irish and the Arab breeding operations. Soviet Song had been the Clubs most famous flat horse; winning a scarcely believable six grade ones in the early years of the 21st century. As the 2017 flat season dawned, it became apparent to some that the club might have potentially another superstar on their hands, a filly called Marsha.

Marsha was a four-year-old horse that the Club had bred out of their own mare, Marlinka. The dam had been quite a good horse in her own right for Elite, but now resided as one of the club's broodmares at Oak Lodge stud, in the horse county of Kildare. Marsha, trained in Newmarket by Sir Mark Prescott, had shown enough in her second and third year of racing for the Club to believe they had a seriously quick and precocious talent on their hands. She entered the 2017 season as a horse with an impressive BHA rating of 110 (over a 100 meant she was well above average) and clearly possessed the ability to compete in the season's top class sprints. However, in such a highly competitive division, potential was one thing, competing against the world's bluebloods might be something entirely different.

Marsha outlined her credentials with a season's opening victory at Newmarket in the prestigious Palace stakes in May. Aiden O'Brien, the master trainer associated with one of the Worlds finest training operations, Ballydoyle, saw his highly rated horse Washington DC well beaten. Marsha's achievement was all the more impressive because she became the first horse since Lochsong, many years before, to defy a group one penalty. In other words, she carried more weight and still gave out a beating. It was an impressive performance that saw her rating go up six pounds.

Plans were set for Marsha to take in Royal Ascot in the middle of June, although I took great interest in the trainer's view that this might be followed by a trip to the Curragh in July. Marsha did turn up for the King Stand stakes at Royal Ascot in June and with a gutsy run claimed third place, picking up over £40,000 in prize money. However, as a reminder of what the Elite horse was up against, the impressive winner Lady Aurelia was an American super star in the making and on this day looked a class apart.

Marsha though had lost little in defeat and it appeared was still planning to visit the Curragh in July. I was suitably emboldened to make my travel plans and a visit to Monaghan to see the 'Bull' McCabe was inked in. The precarious nature of attempting to get into the owners' ring in Ireland with Marsha, was soon apparent when in the days before the trip, news filtered through that the trainer was having doubts, particularly in regard to the Irish weather! The recent rains had softened up the Curragh and the Baronet was so concerned that the day before my trip, much to my consternation, Marsha was given an entry at York, on Saturday 15th of July. As I sailed over the Irish Sea, I was less than certain that Elite's top sprinter would be joining me.

God, it would seem, can smile on the righteous! Because as I arrived at Monaghan I was greeted with the news that not only was Marsha declared at the Curragh but my master-plan had once again come off, as I was allocated an owner's badge for the afternoon. It would appear that my 'ownership' caper in Ireland was going to get off the ground at the very top, with a visit to Ireland's premier racecourse as the 'owner' of the marvellous Marsha.

***

RACE DAY - MARSHA AT THE CURRAGH, SATURDAY, JULY 15, 2017
THE RACECOURSE

The Curragh, as all the race books tell you, is Ireland's premier flat racing course; it is often referred to as Ireland's Newmarket. Situated on the Curragh plain in County Kildare, it can be found between the towns of Newbridge and Kildare. I had been a couple of times before, indeed I had attended last year's Irish Derby when the grand old racecourse was packed to the rafters, as the well fancied Harzand won in some style. Following the victory, I watched as the dignitaries handed over the trophy amongst much pomp and an opera singer belted out the Curragh of Kildare. It all seemed very appropriate and whetted my appetite for what this visit might bring.

However the Curragh in the July of 2017 was very different, as the course was undergoing major renovation. The main stand from which I had watched the Derby had been demolished and there were a set of temporary stands alongside the final furlongs. Apparently this whole renovation had sparked some controversy, with many in Ireland feeling that some of the Irish classics should not be run at HQ, while it was undergoing such renovation. The Curragh had withstood the criticism and the Irish Oaks that was on today's card was one of the six classics that were all being run at the changing Curragh. I was delighted that they had taken this line, even in its reduced circumstances, being inside the ring with 'your' horse at the Curragh, was very much the plan.

Despite the changes at the Curragh, the treatment of the 'owners' at the old course was the best I have ever experienced (and that includes Long champ, on Arc day). Arriving at reception, I was accorded all the usual pleasantries as they passed on all the complimentary cards to use in the owners' lounge. They even made a fuss of the Bull and he was given complimentary admittance as my guest.

Unfortunately, I couldn't get Bull into the owners' lounge at this point and while he went off to grab a sausage roll, I was entertained with a lavish two-course meal of the highest quality. Feeling in an opulent mood, I passed on the Tipperary beef and opted for the Atlantic monkfish with crispy pancetta heirloom, tomato ragout, and sweet potato and pistachio bon bon. The served desert consisted of dark and milk chocolate delice, raspberries with chocolate soil and Chantilly cream. It would be fair to say that it beat biscuits and tea at a cold Bangor on Dee in October!

I was informed, that as I was the 'owner' with the English horse (i.e. not one of the home country's horses) I was entitled to use the owners' lounge throughout the afternoon and not just at the time of my race. I cheered the Bull up, when we met with this news, saying I could get him a cup of tea! Outside the owners' lounge it was a perfectly pleasant late afternoon, which was verging on an Irish heat wave, in that despite the cloud cover, there was enough heat behind the cloud to remove one's jacket! The cool wind though meant this was a short-term move. Because of the renovation, the crowd was less than would normally have been here on Oaks day, but this meant there was enough room to move about, look at the horses in the paddock and take one's seat in the temporary stand. Although there was a narrow walkway between the stand and the parade ring, most people were managing the task well. Even in its reduced circumstances, one can take on board just what an important place the Curragh is to the Irish.

Horses have been racing on this spring lush turf since the 1700s; the massive space of nearly 5000 acres is not just made up of the green space used for racing. The military have long had an involvement, in Ireland's turbulent history, most students would know of the Curragh incident, when in 1914 there was a proto mutiny, when British soldiers failed to follow orders in the face of the home rule movement. Following Michael Collins treaty in 1921, the land passed from the British Crown to the Irish minister for finance and later the minister of Defence. As the nascent State took control over its historic racing area, one can track the various improvements made to the course, which to some extent have gone hand in hand with the maturity of the Irish state within the EU. Now it awaits its latest development, the £65 million redevelopment that hoped to open in 2019.

For today though, the Bull and myself were positioned in the temporary stand, able to see down the five furlongs that would be the distance that Marsha would race over in the fourth race on the card. The lush, wide course shows a gentle undulation and a clear uphill finish. The Bull was on good punting form and had already bagged two winners, when I joined him with the winner of the third race.

At that point I hurried down from the stand and made my way to the owners enclosure to acquaint myself with the other Elite 'owners' present at the Curragh.

***

PRE RACE

I was quickly into the ring, where I recognised a Scottish chap I had met in the ring at Longchamp. Initially we were the only Elite 'owners' present, but our numbers soon swelled with a gathering of around a dozen people, discussing where we had all come from and what we thought of 'our' horse's chances.

Sir Mark Prescott wasn't at the course and instead had sent his assistant the quietly spoken William Butler. Given my Irish 'ownership' plans, I was in a somewhat bizarre situation. Initially the plan was just to try and get some 'runners' at Irish racecourses, but here I was at the Curragh with a horse that was 4/7 on, in other words considered by the bookmakers to be a certainty to win. So one had moved from being happy just to have a runner to wondering where the winner's presentation stand was located! I would have to say, I wasn't happy with having such an overwhelming favourite, as most punters know there are no certainties in horse racing. The reason that Marsha was such a hot favourite, other than her outstanding form was the fact that Lady Aurelia had swerved the race, and the other big threat in the division, Battaash had done likewise.

William Butler was courteous and informative, telling us that Marsha had taken the voyage over the Irish Sea in her stride and had eaten up well at breakfast. The rains had stayed away and William was happy with the going. I got the distinct impression that if William were 'on' a certainty in a race, it would never have been his style to shout it from the rooftops. He did quietly express the view that with one or two of the big stars missing from the race, there might be a lack of pace. This could be important for Marsha, as she tended to run her best races by coming off a fast pace and passing those horses in front.

It was a small field of six horses but there was enough quality there to suggest that Marsha would need to be at her best to win. It would have been foolish to write off any horse trained by the brilliant A P O'Brien, but surely Alphabet, representing the all, powerful John Magnier axis, was not in Marsha's class. On ratings alone the Irish triumvirate of Ardhoomey, Spirit Quartz and Hit The Bid, had a lot to find to trouble 'our' horse. Perhaps, fellow British horse Caspian Prince represented the greatest danger. This horse was a prolific handicap winner and had recently won the Epsom dash for a third time. However, the very fact that his victories were at handicap level meant that he would be facing a tough task in a superior group race such as the Sapphire Stakes.

By the time we had watched Marsha stride around the parade ring a few times, Luke Morris, our jockey appeared. Luke is one of the quieter jockeys, being relatively undemonstrative when he is riding, although I feel he possesses that single minded determination that often distinguishes the very top men in their profession. He was Marsha's regular jockey and had apparently flown in for the engagement, which we were all very happy about. Characteristically he said little, touching his cap as he went to mount up. Reading the Racing Post, every single tipster went for Marsha, with many indicating it was a formality. The Racing Post verdict summed up our sense of destiny; "Marsha is making good strides at being the second best five furlong sprinter around and her third to Lady Aurelia at Ascot showed that she is very close to having that honour. She should take this in her stride…" Clearly there was little value to be had at the prohibitive odds, but a big note went on all the same, although I did have a slight feeling of unease at being on such an overwhelming favourite.

***

THE RACE – SAPHIRE STAKES (GROUP TWO) 5 FURLONGS

I trained the binoculars onto the bottom of the hill, to see Marsha break well and sit comfortably in second place after a furlong. Caspian Prince was making the running and had opened up a comfortable lead at the halfway stage, with the others in pursuit. Inside the final quarter of a mile, Luke Morris asked her for an effort and she fairly effortlessly drew up level sides with the leader. At this point it looked as though her momentum would take her into a significant lead, but Caspian Prince was proving to be a stubborn opponent and maintained his efforts. The horses were neck and neck as they approached the finishing line, with Marsha seeming to my eyes to be marginally in front. At the line both horses shot through together and a photograph was immediately called for to determine the winner. There was no question this was a tight finish, the Bull was pessimistic on her chances and when we saw the photograph still it showed that Caspian Prince had his head down at the line, to win by the narrowest of margins.

***

POST RACE

It's always disappointing when a horse loses what seems on ratings alone to be a certain victory, but that is what makes racing the spectacle it is. There was clearly some disappointment among the 'owners' when we recongregated back in the ring. Many had been anticipating photographs on the winner's platform and champers in the owners' lounge, but instead we congregated by the second place pole and waited for William to join us. Luke Morris obviously on a tight schedule had already disappeared. One or two members thought this might have been a reality check for 'our' horse, one of those closest to me murmured that she should have won that, if she was going to compete in this division. The deflation soon passed and one of the 'owners' boldly stated that Marsha had already spoilt us, and that you can take nothing for granted in racing. The Curragh didn't appear to be Marsha's lucky course, as she had lost here a year ago and perusal of the photo showed that 'our' horse's head was in front just before the line and just after. I asked William what he thought, and he reiterated that they weren't totally happy with the way the race had been run and that Luke had emphasised to him that there had not been enough pace in the race to play to Marsha's strengths. As a true Gentleman, he repeated there is no certainties in racing and that Caspian Prince had run a very shrewd race.

I was very sanguine about the situation, after all I had come all this way for 'my' first Irish runner and she could have been running at York! Marsha and Elite had enabled me to have a brilliant day at Ireland's premier flat course, who wouldn't be happy with that. Taken at this initial stage of the Irish 'ownership' project, this did seem to be the one cast iron chance of having a winner, it didn't work out that way, maybe a less favoured horse might surprise me further down the line.

The Marsha story though wasn't finished and would take some amazing turns before finishing back here in Ireland.

To some extent she had some questions to answer in her next race at Goodwood in early August. In the King George stakes the other 'talking' horse in the division Battaash appeared, and in a blistering exhibition of pace obliterated the field, beating Marsha in third place by three lengths. Marsha remained consistent and picked up another good 'pot', but now there were two sprinters that looked outside her league.

That was certainly how the bookmakers saw it, as all three horses finally lined up together at the end of August to compete in the group 1 Nunthorpe Stakes at York. It was billed as a two horse race, with Marsha freely available at the generous odds of 8/1. The media pundits drooled over the clash between the two speed merchants, virtually ignoring 'our' homebred. Once the race started, Lady Aurelia under the ebullient Frankie Dettori broke smartly and Battaash (who had been agitated before the start) set off in furious pursuit. Marsha, initially trailed in the pack, but she appeared to be travelling strongly and with the fast pace that suited her was placed to mount a challenge. As she moved into contention, Battaash looked a spent force and fell away, but the American filly was still going well on the other side of the track. Marsha though had the momentum, and with each stride she ate into Lady Aurelia's lead, so that both horses flashed past the post together. In one of the season's indelible moments, Frankie Detttori punched the air, convinced he had won the race. However, the photo-finish camera begged to differ and a few moments later it was announced Marsha had got up to win on the line, by the proverbial 'nose'

It was a sweet moment for the understated Morris, as the dazed Dettori was left to contemplate all the next day's Newspaper pictures of his premature celebration. So it would seem that the Curragh experience had merely been a scene setter for Marsha, as she recorded her second and the Elite Club's eighth Group One victory. Marsha had arrived and beaten both the expensive superstars, not bad for a homebred filly from a race club. The Handicapper responded to one of the season's great races and Marsha was lifted to a rating of 121, one pound higher than the great Soviet Song had recorded in 2004.

The Marsha story rolled on. She returned to the scene of her first Group One victory in France and was a brave second in the L'Abbaye in Chantilly. By winning the Nunthorpe stakes she was given a free entry into the World famous Breeders' Cup in the United States. Although plans were now afoot to sell Marsha, so that she could be retired as a broodmare, the word was that she was a likely runner. So it was that Marsha ran her final race at Del Mar, near San Diego in November. In typical fashion the ultra consistent horse took all the travel and change in her stride to finish a respectable sixth in a race that American horses dominated, typically 'our' horse was the highest finishing non-American horse.

December the second was the final date in Marsha's season as she headed for the Tattersall's sales in Newmarket. Marsha by now was a valuable racehorse, who belied her humble background and was now featured as one of the most attractive acquisitions at the prestigious sales. None of us, who had been her lucky 'owners' at the Curragh, or the wider Elite membership, were aware of her precise value, but we had been told that the 'management' had put a hefty reserve price on our star performer. Elite had sold at the thoroughbred sales before, when the horse I had 'owned' at Longchamp, Ribbons, had accrued over half a million guineas. Now there were realistic expectations that Marsha would bring in at least four times that amount. The actual sales on December the second proved to be as dramatic a theatrical experience as any of Marsha's great races. The bidding had soon topped the two million mark and it became apparent that a monster contest was developing between the two superpowers of bloodstock flat racing; John Magnier's, Coolmore operation of Ireland and Sheikh Mohammed, ruler of Dubai, and owner of the most extensive bloodstock operation in the World. Each bid from the Coolmore man was met by a sharp nod of the head from the Sheikh's representative, as the price escalated above five million guineas! The tension was palpable as the price continued to rise, until the hushed expectancy was broken by a spontaneous burst of applause, as Coolmore's stratospheric bid of six million guineas brought no response and the gavel came down in the Irish superpower's favour. Marsha had broken the European record for a thoroughbred, and would return to Ireland in a permanent capacity.

Christopher McGrath's brilliant book; 'Mr Darley's Arabian', traces the colourful story of the evolution of the world's greatest racehorses, that nearly all come from a male line that can be traced back to the Darley Arabian in 1700. As Mr McGrath puts it; 'each link, in the golden chain of twenty three generations dividing the Darley Arabian and Frankel'. One of those 'links' was Frankel's sire, Galileo. He resides at Coolmore's main farm at County Tipperary and a visit to this stud would cost a small fortune for a few seconds and the prospect of producing the next great horse and 'link' in what McGrath calls; 'thoroughbred's genetic big bang'. It was announced immediately after the Tattersall's sale that Marsha would reside at Coolmore and obviously visit the World's best sire. To complete this genetic cycle, Elite themselves, enriched by their spectacular sale announced that they would send Marlinka (Marsha's dam) to visit the sports most recent superstar Frankel. The breeding cycle was complete, the dreams and aspirations would be maintained.

WHERE TO STAY AND DRINK THE GUINNESS

Myself, and the Bull had decided to take in a bit of bed and breakfast so as to be near the famous racecourse. We decided on The Boyne View, Drinadaly, just outside the pretty and impressive town of Trim. An imposing statue of the Duke of Wellington, is the surprising entrance to the town, he appears to have some family links to the place, probably meaning that he owned most of it many years ago! The Bull is on great form, he has had more than his fair share of illness and family misfortune and yet he remains upbeat and the very best of company. I admire his courage immensely.

The Boyne View proved to be a pleasantly appointed establishment, run with cheerful efficiency by Anthony and Deidre Hoey. Located as the name infers on the River Boyne, and surrounded by acres of countryside, the accommodation offered all that is best in the more intimately appointed Bed and Breakfast establishments. The excellent breakfasts and friendly demeanour of the hosts, meant it can fulfil its boast of being; 'home from home'. Incidentally, in terms of horse breeding it is located next door to the famous William Flood stud.

The small and pretty town of Trim has plenty of attractions, however the standout feature is its Cambro-Norman Twelfth Century castle. A guided tour of its interior is a must, our visit being enlivened by a knowledgeable guide, clearly a well travelled man, as he had a working knowledge of the Manchester beer, Holts! In terms of liquid refreshment, the Hoeys ordered us a taxi for a late night visit to the pubs of Trim, choose carefully as Saturday night can be lively, but the Guinness and traditional music of the James Griffin Pub, hit all the right notes.

The author contemplates the eyelash he 'owns' on the six million guinea horse, Marsha. Curragh July 2017.

3

CULLENTRY, MEATH.

It was whilst in the pretty town of Trim, that my mind moved to the concept of having an Irish trainer for the forthcoming year. Given my English location a syndicate style horse was not a good idea, as I would not be in Ireland on enough occasions to make the proposition worthwhile. A racing club was the answer; a club in theory would run a string of horses and might enable me to see one of the horses run from time to time. Racing Clubs in Ireland appear to be thin on the ground, but there was one I knew of just down the road from our base in Trim at Cullentra stables in County Meath. It belonged to the highly successful and upwardly mobile trainer, Gordon Elliott. Elliott was a man going places; in 2017 he was challenging Willie Mullins, for time in memorial Ireland's top National Hunt trainer, to the blue ribbon of the year's Champion trainer prize. With an apprenticeship served under the doyen of English National Hunt trainers, Nicky Henderson, behind him, he burst to National prominence by winning the English Grand National. Elliott was only twenty-nine in 2007 when Silver Birch won the National at 33/1. Year after year subsequently, he had built up his operation in County Meath, so that eventually it rivalled the pre-eminent Willie Mullins' yard. A measure of his success was illustrated in 2016, when the pantomime villain of Ryan Air, Michael O'Leary, moved many of his highly rated horses from Mullins to Elliott in typically controversial circumstances. Building on his success, Elliott won the prestigious Cheltenham Gold Cup in 2016 with Don Cossack and in 2017 received the finest accolade of being the Cheltenham festival top trainer.

These horses were hardly likely to be running in the racing club colours. By definition, racing club horses were usually cheaply purchased older experienced horses or occasionally young unknown types. The hope was that Elliott's expertise might tease the occasional win from one of the horses and more particularly that these horses might prove to be tough animals that got 'us' to the races on a regular basis. I had my eye on the club for some time as the idea of an Irish trainer germinated, indeed my hesitancy appeared to have cost me, as the annual fee seemed to have increased somewhat. With a changing string of about half a dozen horses, that seemed to run all around Ireland and occasionally win, the club fitted the bill. On this basis, Bull, and myself drove up to the village of Longwood, in Cullentry, County Meath and onto the Elliott stables at Cullentra House. It was a beautiful sunny morning, which allowed us to see that this was a big operation, but little else, as there was security all around which restricted entry. However, I had seen enough and had all the information to make Gordon Elliott 'my' Irish trainer. While I am sure this news meant nothing to the master of Cullentra House or was unlikely to make the breaking news of the Racing Post, it afforded myself a certain satisfaction! Gordon was the man.

On my return to England, I completed the application process, setting up the direct debits that would pay a few hundred pounds to enable me to 'own' a horse in the Country of my parents' birth. The only sticking point had been the issue of obtaining an owner's badge on the occasions when a horse might run. In England where race clubs proliferate, you are often competing with hundreds or even thousands of people to obtain a badge, so therefore your chances are limited. However, after discussion with the Club secretary I was reassured that this was a more bespoke club in terms of numbers and that In Ireland things were more relaxed and that she didn't see me having too many problems obtaining the requisite badges. Time would no doubt tell, but I was lucky with badges and from an economic point of view this was the only way that I was ever likely to be an 'owner' in Ireland without breaking the bank for the privilege.

My decision to join up with Gordon Elliott paid an immediate dividend, as within the month I was sent an invitation to visit the yard on an open day on the first Saturday in September. This enabled me to visit the horses in the string and see the trainer working, at first hand. I subsequently arrived at Cullentra House with Sue, on a sunny Saturday morning, looking around me there was a good turn out of members arriving from all corners, that included Norfolk and London. There was a friendly informal feel to proceedings, as we were allowed to wander around freely, taking in some of the two hundred horses that Elliott trains. The horses included stable stars like Apples Jade along with 'our' own club horses, which at the time appeared to number seven. Training assistant Colm Murphy took us over to the stables that contained some of 'our' horses, and we were able to take plenty of pictures of horses like Dawerann and Bettatogether. The horses seemed relaxed and well turned out.

As we came together after the stable visit, Gordon appeared in our midst and took the group out to the well-appointed gallops, contained within Cullentra House. Some of the horses were to be put through their paces and we took up our positions to see the horses and hear Gordon's thoughts. Gordon struck me as the kind of man who doesn't go in for smooth, long-winded speeches; he was down to earth and clearly in command of this domain. His commentary on the exercising horses was brief and to the point, although one gets the impression that despite the brevity, it might be worth taking note. Once the gallops were completed, we were brought down to a general corral, where all 'our' horses were paraded and this eventually led to a mass photo call. Gordon was typically careful with his comments re the specific horses. Dawerann, had been in the club a couple of years, having previously been trained by Michael Hourigan, he had lots of runs against his name, but not many wins. Urtheoneiwant was another who had been in the club for a bit and the mare had won at Gordon's favourite Scottish course, Perth. Bettatogether, had come from Alan King in England, and with a big injury lay off and little success, the question was could Gordon work the oracle. Some like Ring Ben were eleven years old, without a win to its name, so he might stretch Gordon's magic! But others were young and untried; the four-year-old Shirleys Gold Well was well regarded. There was even a flat horse, Fairy Flute, as Gordon was spreading his wings with impressive wins on the level. The stock phrases were in evidence, a bit of fun it seemed was possible with all and each horse it seemed could have a race in them. My fellow members loved it, their belief in the trainer knew no bounds, if there was improvement to be had in these horses, then Gordon was the man to find it. It seemed to me when a super star like Marsha the six million guineas horse had failed to propel me into the winners' enclosure, that it was very unlikely that any of these horses might manage it. For their moment in the sun to coincide with one of my visits to Ireland was a long shot, but I had learnt over the years that racing could be a funny old game. To be honest I was more concerned with just being able to manage the trick of being there when the horse ran, that would be a victory in itself, anything more than that would be the icing on the cake.

It proved to be an impressive open day, the facilities at Cullentra House were first class and Gordon clearly had a strong army of horses at his disposal. The meeting was rounded off with tea and bacon baps as we mingled with the other members. Sue and I went for a final walk up to the top paddocks where a couple of horses took our eye. On our return the gates were open and the cars were beginning to make their exit, when we turned the corner and ran straight into Mr Elliott. Gordon is an unpretentious down to earth individual and he immediately greeted us and asked us from where we had come. He didn't seem unduly surprised at the distance travelled and asked where we were staying. I congratulated him on the scale and success of his operation. This was a theme he warmed to, pointing out the stable extensions over recent years. Success doesn't seemed to have turned Gordon's head, he struck me as a humble, common sense operator, I reckon his training mantra would be, keep it simple. He impressed me, he was pleasant and approachable and wished us well for the rest of our trip. I shook his hand and wished him well for the rest of the season.

The decision to join Gordon Elliott had paid an immediate dividend with an excellent stable open day and the payback was doubled, as we were due to see our first runners that very afternoon at Navan. Dawerann and Fairy Flute were both entered to race. Just as the secretary had assured me owners' badges were provided and as a further return on my investment we were given discounted tickets to see the races in style from the Proudstone suite. Things were working out very nicely.

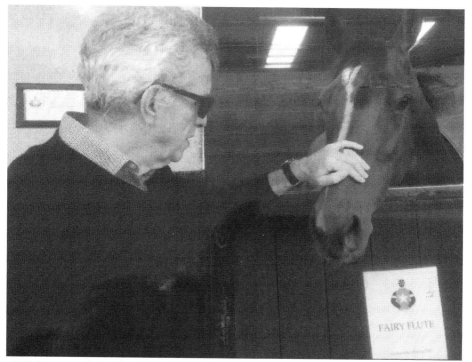

With one of the 'string', Fairy Flute, on visit to Gordon Elliott yard.
September 2017.

4

NAVAN

The delightful concept of two of 'my' horses both appearing on the same card at Navan disappeared mid morning, when it became clear that Fairy Flute had some sort of niggle and wouldn't be taking part. Dawerann though was a definite starter and that was good enough for me. The Proudstone suite was a further bonus, being a spacious lounge area with an extensive balcony that allowed a good view of the course and a direct view of the final furlong to the finishing line. We found a table to study some fiendishly competitive looking races and downed a good quality pint of Guinness at the somewhat prohibitive price of five Euros. Still we were quaffing in style.

Gordon Elliott of course was a top National Hunt trainer, but today's race was going to be on the flat. Fairy Flute had been the flat horse, but she was withdrawn, so Dawerann was carrying the club colours. He was an experienced hurdler but was running today to blow away a few cobwebs and increase his fitness level. Dawerann was no superstar but he seemed the ideal syndicate horse in that he had run in lots of races, on a regular basis and rarely sustained injury. The day's race day programme notes emphasised his durability with sixty completed runs against his name. The three career wins tempered enthusiasm somewhat, but with twenty-two placed efforts and over 40,000 Euro won, he was hardly a hopeless case.

***

RACE DAY – DAWERANN AT NAVAN , SATURDAY, SEPTEMBER 2, 2017
THE RACECOURSE

Navan racecourse is situated at Proudstone in County Meath, some fifty kilometres north of Dublin. They have been racing here since 1920, when a group of local farmers came together to form a racecourse. This tells us something of the importance of racing in Ireland, as this was at the height of the 'troubles'. It is best known for its jumping, but it hosts flat racing as well, as was the case today. It's a left-handed course, with quite wide bends and a stiff uphill finish.

It seemed to me to typify many of the Irish courses that I had visited in the past, in that it was developed on quite a grand scale, with a main grandstand and a set of adjoining suites, of which Proudstone was one. There was a large parade ring away to our right, with quite a few food outlets dotted around. The best of these was to be found under the grandstand, a large cafeteria-style hall, which served substantial meat cuts as part of a reasonably priced roast dinner.

The weather had remained sunny from the fine morning, but the cloud was beginning to build. Torrential rain was forecast, but luckily for us it would not arrive until over night. Despite the pleasant weather and a Saturday race card, the attendance could only be described as sparse. Ireland could have a problem with its race going public, I had seen thin crowds before and outside the big festivals it could be that the sport is losing spectators. The usual culprits of televised racing and alternative activities could be the reason for the problem. Although some race goers I have met feel it is more down to uncompetitive racing, with the Mullins and Elliott teams piling up the winners, there are a profusion of short priced favourites and this in itself is a disincentive.

In any event, a healthy turn out of club members had boosted today's attendance and after struggling to find just one winner on a tricky card, the time grew nearer to the fifth race, the five past four handicap flat race, run over one mile six furlongs. Dawerann's moment had arrived, and as one of twenty-three runners he had his work cut out to make an impression.

***

PRERACE

The race was due to be a typically competitive affair, with lots of flat trained horses appearing to have a chance. As we walked down from our suite to the parade ring, we noticed that Gordon's other horse, High Expectations was favourite and our boy was friendless at 25/1. Even though there were a good number of members drifting down, the secretary was proved to be right, as there was no trouble getting into the 'ring'.

Irish racing it would seem is a very relaxed affair. In fact it was so relaxed here at Navan, that when the time came to enter the ring, there didn't appear to be a steward to flash the badges at. Over a dozen of us congregated towards the centre of the ring. I engaged in a bit of the usual small talk with fellow 'owners', who seemed relatively upbeat about the horse despite its price. I was more circumspect and kept my doubts to myself, all were enjoying being in the ring with 'their' horse. In a quiet moment as we awaited our trainer, I looked to my right and standing just feet away was the famous Irish flat trainer, John Oxx, standing totally on his own. The last time I had seen John Oxx in the ring, I was staring through the binoculars at one of Ireland's premier trainers, at the Curragh for the Irish Oaks in 1997. That day he was training what was to be his first winner of the famous race, a horse called Ebadiyla. Running in my 'lucky colours' of the Aga Khan, and with Johnny Murtagh on board, they became my 'go to' selection every time I raced in Ireland. They never seemed to let me down either; horse race betting seemed so less complicated then! John Oxx had maintained a high profile through the noughties training perhaps his greatest racehorse, Sea the Stars, to many triumphs. To be honest, I thought he had now retired, but it would appear that despite Aidan O'Brien's total dominance of Irish flat racing, he was still on the go. Apparently he was enjoying something of a renaissance, about to train what all trainers were hoping would be the lottery ticket to future success, foals from the great Frankel. Today, his horse Kozy was down at the Dawerann end of the betting market, but I did note that one tipster fancied it. I had always felt that John Oxx offered a certain ecclesiastical air to the hurly burly of horse racing. Today, I kept a respectful distance.

By now Gordon had appeared, of course having more than one horse in the race he was dividing his time between owners. He was more formally attired now having dispensed with the jeans and trainers from the morning session. Dawerann, continued to drift in the market, now reaching 33/1. Still Dawerann didn't know his odds were drifting and looked relaxed and well turned out as he plodded around the ring, enabling members to snap away happily. Gordon's view was that Dawerann was an unpredictable horse, 'he could run a stinker' or maybe 'grab some place money', was his assessment. Gary Haplin, now joined us, he was a young aspiring Irish jockey, other than touching his cap he remained silent. He wasn't saying much, but he was listening intently to his gaffer's final instructions. Once loaded up Gary and Dawerann departed the ring and we began to make our way back to the suite. I didn't really think Dawerann had much chance, but loyalty dictated a bet, however I put a more sizeable amount on High Expectations. After all, we were all in the same team!

***

THE RACE – HANDICAP 1 MILE 6 FURLONG

With this being a flat race starter stalls were employed. Dawerann, showed some unfamiliarity with the process by staying in his stall, while all the other horses raced away. In what seemed to be a couple of seconds later, Dawerann lurched out of his stall and began the pursuit of the other horses. Dawerann took most of the first circuit to catch up with the others and eventually began to pass a couple, settling towards the rear of the field. Needless to say High Expectations was at the other end of the pack, contesting the leadership, as they passed us at the half way stage of the race. As the second circuit unfolded our boy started to make some modest progress, but remained a good way behind the leaders. With two furlongs to go, High Expectation took the lead and Dawerann moved into the midfield of packed horses. It was looking like the race would give me a reasonable payback as High Expectations surged for the finishing line, only to be caught out by the uphill finish and was passed by Lucca to lose by a head. Dawerann finishing well grabbed thirteenth place of the twenty-four runners, a respectable finish given that disastrous start.

***

POST RACE

As we wandered back to the parade ring, we could see that Gordon was engaged with the owners of High Expectations, no doubt commiserating over the close defeat. He eventually made his way over to the club 'owners' and seemed relatively upbeat about Dawerann's performance. He reckoned he had kept going well and had showed the right attitude. The members concurred with this view; the run would sharpen him up for the challenges ahead, seemed to be the conclusion. Gordon added that the first of these challenges would be at Perth, later in the month. With that we began to make our way out of the ring. As we did so we passed by the happy owners of Lucca, who were taking their prize and getting ready for the photographs. Maybe one day, that will be us with an Elliott horse, I thought.

Gordon was true to his word and Dawerann along with Urtheoneiwant both appeared at Perth in late September in the Glorious Finale meeting. It wasn't Ireland, but we were there with complimentary owner's badges at the pretty Scottish course. There was a good turn out of fellow members in Scotland, this was Gordon's favourite course over the water and with a strike rate of twenty seven percent, one can see why. It was all very relaxed once more and I asked Gordon what the horses chances were, he left me in no doubt that place money was the objective. Urtheoneiwant, was up against it in a chase, but stayed on her hooves to collect the minimum prize. Dawerann, looking just as relaxed as at Navan, looked fine walking around the parade ring and with champion jockey Richard Johnson on board, there was a quiet confidence that he might get a place. There were only six other competitors and he was hurdling now, but after a bright start he ran out of steam, finishing fifth. Both horses had brought back some prize money and hopefully it paid for their travel over the Irish Sea. It was a grand day out and further evidence that the Irish horses with Gordon Elliott was proving to be a shrewd move.

WHERE TO STAY AND DRINK THE GUINNESS

This is a bit of a cheat, as we didn't stay at Navan. I am sure the town has many fine hostelries, but I wasn't in a position to make comment. Because the Navan racing was part of a bigger trip, the base once more was the charming town of Trim.

The three stars Castle Arch hotel, situated on the outskirts of the town proved an excellent base. Not to be confused with its slightly upmarket cousin the Castle Hotel, the Castle Arch had a homely feel and produced a typically hearty full Irish breakfast. Although we would look for the Guinness a little further afield, the all night porter must be commended for keeping the bar open and the Guinness flowing, even though our party were the only people left at the bar! We did eat at the Castle hotel and were impressed by an enterprising menu and some good quality food. There are many good Guinness stops in Trim but McCormack's bar facing Trim castle generally won the highest plaudits. As a further equine inducement it appears to be the watering hole for many of the Gordon Elliott stable staff.

Stood next to John Oxx, but keeping a 'respectful distance', Dawerann in the background. Navan September 2017.

5

Laytown

Laytown races would be on many racegoers' 'bucket list', at least for those of a romantic persuasion. Laytown, just North of Dublin is unique with just one day's racing annually along the sands of Laytown strand. I had been racing on the sands before in Ireland, taking in a day in the far west at Achill Island, but Laytown are the 'official' races, recognised by the Irish Race Board. Indeed they have raced horses here for over a century, with very few interruptions. Situated in County Meath, it is just thirty miles from Dublin and has a convenient station on the busy Dublin to Belfast rail line. Although for this the 2017 meeting, Sue had driven us here from our base at Trim and we were accompanied by the distinguished racegoers Mr M and Mr J.

Racing was first recorded here in 1876 and as usual its origins appeared to be linked to the enterprise of a local parish priest. He initially organised the meeting and would have continued in the same vein, had it not been for what John Welcome called the arrival of a 'new and puritanically minded Bishop that put an end to his activities'. Clearly the seed that the priest had sown established itself well enough as Laytown developed a certain historical durability. Racing seemed to continue whatever Ireland's difficulty, with the races continuing for much of the First World War and through the war of independence. By my reckoning we were about to attend the 124th meeting.

The times of the races is controlled by the tides. Once high tide has receded on the nominated day, a small army of staff and volunteers set about establishing the course. Ann Holland talks of the sand being 'scuffed with a seaweed machine' over its whole length and 'flagged out' before crucially 'the damming of the surface' so that water cannot encroach onto the course.

Laytown has enjoyed an eventful history, but as John Welcome points out that, 'although it's no proving ground for classic hopes, it maintains its own standards'. English trainers are not averse to sending their runners here and today Jamie Osborne was represented by a number of runners. Even the great Mr Elliott had recent runners at the course, but he wasn't bothering today and none of the club horses were in evidence. From what I can gather the racecourse has been modified in recent years on account of some controversial races in the past. In years gone by the races had featured a lot more horses, which would run over a more circular route, with some spectators positioned rather precariously on high ground along the course. 1994 appeared to be the year that brought greatest controversy, as general mayhem was brought about, that saw a horse killed and a jockey seriously injured. Since then a stricter regime has been in place, which quite correctly has placed the safety of horse, jockey and spectator as paramount.

On the basis of this, no three-year-old horses are allowed to run, it is now a straight six-furlong course and there is a maximum of ten horses per race. For some time the races have taken place in September and this is to avoid the mass crowds that might swamp the course in the summer. Although looking around, we seemed to be pretty near to full capacity.

We were blessed with good weather, not something one should ever take for granted in the Emerald Isle, the day was characterised by the sun occasionally popping through the cloud, with an appropriate seaside breeze. Parking was to be found in a large field, located close to the railway station. We were in plenty of time, the first race was not due off until five past five, so we had time for a couple of pints of Guinness in the pubs in the village. The pleasant weather had meant there was plenty of room inside the pub, where a fair few different accents attested to the fact that racegoers had come from far and wide. I ran into a chap who had travelled from Cambridge, who was visiting the course for the same reason as us. Clearly a gentleman of the turf, he reckoned he had a live tip for the fifth race, passed on from a man in the know. Shepherd's Purse was the nominated horse and needless to say later in the evening we all backed the animal. We didn't really notice it in running, but it came in eventually, in fourth place. It is about half a mile from the village to the course and we joined the crowds making their way down to Laytown racecourse.

THE RACECOURSE

Given that this is only an annual event, the racecourse is bound to have a somewhat transitory layout. It remains, as it always was, a three-acre field, located on the top of the sand dunes. Close to the entrance, away to the right was a small parade ring and just behind that were three buildings, which housed, the weighing room, the secretary's office and a first aid tent. There were the usual toilet blocks and food vendors with quite large queues already in line. The bookmakers as always were prominent; with a centre pitch in front of some tote offices. There was a tented bar close to the bookmakers and even at this early stage a raucous atmosphere was developing. I was certainly grateful that any imbibing had been done earlier in the afternoon, getting into the tent would have been a challenge, getting out of it again, might have been one hurdle too far!

The race programme, purchased at the gate was bright and relatively informative, although Mr M bemoaned the lack of any real form, on which to base his bets. A bookies benefit was his overview of the forthcoming races, an uneven struggle that he finally gave up on after the fifth race! I decided to trust my luck and generally back horses that had run at the unique venue before. This of course was an eminently sensible move on my part, unfortunately let down by the fact that it only reduced the fields by about 10%.

In many respects, Laytown was the classic country course, as John Welcome writing many years before summarised: 'a carnival style day out for the locals and visitors from further afield'. However any notions of the rustic outback were dispelled by the presence of the corporate tent, at the far end of the course. Here away from the hoi polloi, the white tablecloths billowed in the breeze and the sentry on the door was clearly intent on keeping non-badge holders out. The 'prawn sandwich brigade' to quote a famous Irish sportsman, are, it would seem, to be found everywhere. The majority of the spectators were located in the enclosure positioned on the top of the dune. There were some concrete steps that lead to a terrace, which allowed the spectators to space themselves out, affording them a good view of the strand that stretched out below them. It is still possible to actually get down onto the beach and see the races at close quarters. To do this you need to pass through a turnstile, something we did after the second race.

The terrace layout and visibility for the spectators was pretty good. All that was required now was to watch the races and hopefully grab a winner and stop the adventure becoming the bookies benefit so dreaded by Mr M.

THE RACES

As a spectacle the races are impressive. The horses start from stalls, which are positioned in the middle distance some six furlongs from the finishing line. With the sea away to the left of the starting stalls and the straight sands ahead, it was quite a spectacular scene. The horses quickly covered the ground on the sound surface, the occasional horse missing the break from the stalls, but generally they come in your direction almost in a line. The races last no more than a couple of minutes, usually with a group of horses fighting out some tight finishes. The horses seem to be of a similar quality and the racing was competitive, finding a winner was not going to be easy.

For the third race, Sue and myself went down onto the sands, to see the racing close up. The key to this manoeuvre was to make sure that you have selected your horse and got your bet on before you pass through the turnstile, as given the crowds passing through the gate, getting back up to the terrace was not an option. All betting methodology had now gone 'out the window' and I plumped for 'lucky number' seven, Silk Cravat. Ger Lyons was an established trainer with a good reputation, so his horse Silk Cravat was actually favourite, but given what had happened to the favourites in the first two races, nothing could be taken for granted. If you come to Laytown, you must get down and view at least one of the races from the sands, it is the essence of this racing occasion. The rattling of the hooves over the sands as the horses come towards you and then past almost in a blur was quite spectacular. We had positioned ourselves by the picket fencing about two furlongs from the finish, towards the 'business end' of the contest. It was at this point that the main contenders would make their challenge as they attempted to steal a lead and then hold onto it, as they approached the finish. It was a great spot to take a photograph of the action unfolding, and while I'm no David Bailey, I was pleased with my snap.

As they passed us, Silk Cravat had just moved into the lead, with Live Twice and Haraaz in close pursuit. Horse and jockey were straining every sinew as they tried to gain the crucial advantage. The horses became a blur as they travelled away from us and towards the winning line, to be honest as they finished I couldn't be certain which horse had won. Any doubts soon dissipated as the announcer boomed out that the winner was number seven! The prize money was not to be sniffed at, with over seven thousand Euros to the winner, a figure significantly greater than on offer in low-grade races in the UK.

It was arguably harder for me to get back and observe the prize giving, than it was for Silk Cravat to win the race. Firstly one had to navigate the long queues at the turnstile to return to the terrace above and then carefully manoeuvre between the bookies calling the new race and the beer tent, which appeared to have reached a peak of bacchanalian excess. By the time I reached the parade ring the main prizes had been given out, but Silk Cravat was still there, looking tired but unbowed. Jamie Osborne, who had trained the runner up, was wandering around in a brightly coloured blazer and some officials looked busy as they raced between groups. A photographer was roaming around taking photographs of connections and two aspiring models, who looked strangely out of place as their ten-inch heels sunk into the sodden ground. As the programme had noted;' a trophy of no intrinsic value' had been handed out and then it was on with the next race. There was no more joy to be had on the punting front, as Mr M had pointed out, winners had been hard to find. He consoled himself with a burger and chips, Mr J looked sanguine and Mrs C geared herself up for the journey back to Trim.

POST RACE

We marched away from the course, with a relatively orderly crowd. Many were stopping off at the Laytown pubs, which were still doing good business. I was glad we had done Laytown, it's a one off, well worth doing at least once on a racing odyssey around Ireland. We were blessed with fine weather, and some competitive racing set to a spectacular backdrop.

GUINNESS GUIDE

Gina's Cottage Inn was a perfectly pleasant pub, which satisfied all our needs before the races. Due to the good weather, we had plenty of room inside, which is pleasantly furnished. The Guinness was of a perfectly acceptable standard.

'I'm no David Bailey, but'...Silk Cravat, on the way to winning on the sands. Laytown September 2017.

6

FAIRYHOUSE

In contrast to Navan where I hoped that two of 'my' horses might be on the same card, that trick was achieved at Fairyhouse in June 2018. I had travelled over to Ireland during the record heat wave that had enveloped all of the British Isles. I was hoping to see 'my' horses run at both Fairyhouse and DownPatrick within the same week, as three horses were entered at the two meetings.

Gordon Elliott had enjoyed an inspired run of form in 2018, having already been the leading trainer at the prestigious Cheltenham festival in March and followed that up by winning the English Grand National with a horse called Tiger Roll. It had proved a wise decision on my part to align myself with his fortunes, as his rise to the top of the training ranks from a betting perspective was proving somewhat lucrative. My chief aim all along was to see 'my' horses run in Ireland on a few occasions and who knows maybe even see one of them turn out in the West. Owning a racehorse is an unattainable dream for many, to have a horse run in your colours for a high profile trainer would cost a small fortune, this therefore was the classic shoestring method of bringing the dream about. I was delighted that Dawerann had already obliged in that context at Navan last September and now I was hoping that a couple more might appear at one of Irelands premier racecourses.

The autumn of 2017 and the early part of 2018 provided some wet and unpleasant weather, which together with the vagaries of form or injury had meant we had few runners and little success. This didn't concern me unduly; given the distances involved, I was glad to get the winter over before returning to Ireland for some racing action.

Gordon was adept at changing the equine numbers and by mid 2018 two new horses had been introduced that happened to be the ones I was due to see at Fairyhouse. Smiling Eliza and Scealai Aonair were the two newcomers and they duly brought about a change of fortune for the club. Scealai Aonair was first on board, coming from the well-regarded flat trainer Dermot Weld's yard in April. Despite the fact Gordon had made his name as a jumps trainer, he did have a few flat horses that he was racing with characteristic success. Scealai Aonair had showed some promise in her last race for Weld, finishing third, and Gordon immediately sent her to Clonmel at the start of May.

I sat down to watch the one mile flat race, as I had in virtually all the other races with not a great deal of confidence, but dutifully placed my nominal stake. Just as had occurred with a number of club horses in previous races, the starting price for the horse began to plummet alarmingly in the minutes before the off. It didn't seem to put Scealai Aonair off, as she set off in very determined fashion contesting an early lead with two other horses, looking fresh and full of running. However, I had seen the odd club horse start well before and then fade quickly so I braced myself for tiredness to set in, and the cavalry to pass her as they reached the final bend. Instead much to my surprise, the horse reasserted her authority, bursting clear from the others to pass the winning post in style. At last one of 'my' horses had won a race and we had pocketed 'our' share of over six thousand Euros. Normal service was resumed sixteen days later when she ran down the field at Navan, but she was burdened with more weight and showed a willing attitude. More to the point one of 'my' horses was a winner and as an extra bonus she was declared at Fairyhouse and I would be there to see 'our' winner.

As with London buses, no sooner had one horse won for us, than a second horse Smiling Eliza achieved the same feat. This was another horse, which at least initially would run on the flat, and she had arrived from Gordon's main string of horses. There was little in her profile to suggest we had a winner on our hands although there was some promise in a debut run that left her sixth of sixteen runners at Gowran Park. Mr Elliott was clearly impressed with that run and immediately entered her to race at Navan seven days later. The horse wasn't fancied, being freely available at 16/1. However, as if catching the vibe from Scealai Aonair, Smiling Eliza set off with a flourish, racing to the front of a contested field. Her enthusiasm was unmistakable as she set out to dominate the field, running from the front and as they say not seeing another horse, to win in some style. With another six thousand Euros in the bank and a very nice each way bet pocketed, one could only have the happiest of thoughts regarding 'our' club horses and the utmost respect for 'our' miraculous trainer.

More to the point Gordon had now declared 'our' second winner would run at Fairyhouse. The Irish racehorse on a shoestring project was exceeding expectations; two horses with 'live' chances on a beautiful summer's night at Fairyhouse.

***

RACEDAY – SMILING ELIZA and SCEALAI AONAIR AT FAIRYHOUSE,
FRIDAY, JUNE 15, 2018
THE RACECOURSE

Fairyhouse, just thirteen miles North of Dublin is one of Ireland's premier racecourses and home to the Irish Grand National. A right handed undulating course, it was famous for its challenging fences in the Irish Grand National, but today it would feature a flat card. It is used to capacity crowds of over 25,000 during its Easter Festival, but on this pleasant summer's evening it was deserted. On my travels, Irish race crowds seem to vary from full capacity to empty, and tonight there could only have been a couple of hundred spectators at most. However, this allowed myself and Bull plenty of space to examine the course. They appear to have constructed a new owners' lounge positioned over the weighing room, this was a pleasant airy room affording a view of the parade ring and serving food that appeared to be of a higher quality than that available from the vendors on course.

It was while I was enjoying my coffee and biscuits that a man in a blue Fairyhouse blazer welcomed me and asked what horse I was with. I assumed he was the meet and greet man and he was certainly doing a good job, as he was a typically charming and friendly presence. He was particularly impressed that I was with Gordon, who he seemed to have a very high opinion of and it transpired that Gordon had trained horses for this chap in the past. Indeed this charming fellow had been in a syndicate that had owned a horse that had won the National at this very course. When I enquired where the Guinness was to be located, my host then marched me over to the old owners' suite located in the Powers Gold Label stand. On the way into the bar we wandered along a corridor that had framed pictures of all the Grand National winners on the wall, we stopped proudly by a picture of his horse, Davys Lad, for an impromptu photo shoot. Thanking him for all his help, I settled down with Bull for a slightly overpriced pint of Guinness served in a plastic pint pot, and surveyed what looked to be a difficult looking race card.

Fairyhouse must be quite a sight when full to capacity on Easter Monday, but today one had to use one's imagination. There was the characteristic large scale stands (Powers and Jameson) to watch the racing, which from what I could see were standing only. As everywhere these days corporate needs were well catered for with a suite of rooms on the top of the stands that afforded panoramic views of the course. The ground floor incorporates the usual mix of bars, cafeteria and tote outlets. It was in this area that I came across an impressive wooden board that lists all those winners of the Irish Grand National, listing Arkle (perhaps Ireland's most famous race horse) and his victory in 1964. He may have won it just the once, but his stellar reputation based on his exploits when trouncing the English champion at the Cheltenham festival was set in stone. The pictures of 'himself' and Pat Taaffe are to be found at all points up the stairway to the old owners lounge. Fairyhouse is an impressive racecourse, built on the kind of scale that reflects the importance of the horse in Irish culture.

***

PRE RACE

The weather had turned a little overcast and it was raining when Smiling Eliza appeared for the penultimate race on the card at 8.20. It was easy to spot my fellow 'owners'' as we were the only 'crowd' in a quiet parade ring. Gordon appeared in our midst, making a typically downbeat introduction and some concise comments about the horse. The gist of his commentary was that he was pleased with Eliza, she had run well in recent races but she was now in a much tougher contest and would have to run to her best to be involved at the business end of the race. She was nonetheless carrying bottom weight and this might help in a tight handicap. There were other good horses in the race that had won more races than our girl and Bolger's Scoil Naisiunta was a warm favourite, but Smiling Eliza was vying for second favourite trading at around 4/1. The Racing Post thought her a strong candidate commenting that she would be 'hard to contain' over the distance. We were certainly an optimistic bunch of 'owners" as our jockey Wayne Lordon appeared, took instruction from Gordon and jumped onto Smiling Eliza. 'Our' horse seemed relaxed and was certainly well turned out as she circled around us before heading out to the starting post.

Could this be the elusive winner in Ireland? A surprising candidate to achieve what Marsha couldn't manage at the Curragh. I was suitably emboldened and placed a large bet.

***

THE RACE – HANDICAP 1 MILE 4 FURLONGS

We had a clear view from the terraces of the Powers stand, although I was surprised to see no large television screen on the course. I had to make do with the TV sets inside the lounge to check on the pre race activities and Smiling Eliza went into the starting stalls with no problems. From these Eliza broke well and took up a prominent position racing with the pacesetters in third position. Racing confidently she took closer order to the front two as the horses reached the half way stage and the dream victory began to look a distinct possibility. As they reached the vital final corner bend, Wayne began to ask the horse for an increased effort. Smiling Eliza responded well and was in real contention with three or four horses as they began to race up the final straight. But then in a trice the race was run, as accelerating from the back Total Demolition swept by all the leaders, winning the race and leaving the others to fight over the finishing places. Smiling Eliza battled on gamely to finish a tired horse in fourth place.

***

POST RACE

I was slightly deflated when we reconvened in the parade ring by the fourth place pole. Smiling Eliza had been a fancied runner and if truth were told she had never really threatened the main protagonists. Being run out of third place meant my each way wager had gone down and the six hundred and twenty five Euro prize money was a reflection on the paltry amounts available for owners and trainers alike.

However the reception committee of owners gathering around Gordon seemed pleased enough as a tired looking horse returned to our midst. A 'good effort' was the consensus and Gordon, who was circumspect before the race, deemed himself satisfied. She had run a good race was his verdict and as he had predicted the extra weight had been a factor in slowing her down at the finish.

No sooner had the post mortem ended than all our thoughts immediately turned to our other runner, Scealai Aonair, who was of course due to run in the very next race, so we had no reason to vacate the ring, instead we stood around making small talk as we awaited 'our' second runner. Scealai was not as fancied as Eliza and was one of twenty-one runners, in what looked a fiendishly difficult handicap. My confidence dipped a little further when Gordon told us he couldn't stop for this race, but would listen to it on the radio. The top weight Schoolboy Error seemed to set the standard and Shane Nolan's horse was a warm favourite.

Scealai, courtesy of the win in her penultimate race had to carry second top weight and the going and distance were apparently not in her favour. She seemed calm enough as she paraded around in front of her band of 'owners', this time little was said as we dispersed to the grandstand to see what she could do in the night's final race.

***

THE RACE – HANDICAP 1 MILE 4 FURLONGS

There was something of a cavalry charge from the starting stalls in the middle distance and I was struggling to see where Scealai Aonair was but the commentator called her name as one of the early leaders. With the binoculars now trained on her, I was able to monitor a good start as she kept up with the pacemakers over the first four furlongs. It was a tightly contested race and Scealai managed to hold her position in about seventh until they turned into the straight, where there was a perceptible change of pace. As the pace quickened Scealai began to tire and almost immediately the horses massing behind her began to accelerate past our tiring steed. Although she bravely maintained her effort all the way to the line, her finishing position was fourteenth in a race won by Schoolboy Error.

***

POST RACE

It was a tired horse that returned to the pre parade area and there were a few 'owners' present to greet Scealai in a rapidly emptying Fairyhouse. Not much can be said when a horse runs down the field, but 'owners' seem to usually see some positives in these situations and the run was considered to have been a good education for 'our' gallant girl. The extra weight and the firm going were clearly against her, there would be other days no doubt, probably when more typically Irish weather reappeared.

I was sanguine about the race, I was a pleased 'owner', both horses had got me to Fairyhouse and the next day I got the report that they had eaten up well and were enjoying a roll in the field. Job done!

WHERE TO STAY AND DRINK THE GUINNESS

The elegant village of Slane, just twenty minutes from Fairyhouse is a good location to stop. It is an obvious stopping point as it is located at the intersection of the N2 Dublin to Derry road and the N51 Drogheda to Navan road. A picturesque and historic, eighteenth century village, that offers much to the discerning visitor. The World heritage site of Newgrange is not far away, although we satisfied our interests with a quick visit to the Hill of Slane. This is situated just to the north of the village, a healthy walk or a five-minute drive. The remarkably well-preserved old monastery site has association with Ireland's patron saint, Patrick. It was here that he lit the first Pascal fire in 433 AD and when you ramble through the remains you can find the fenced in statue of Saint Patrick, surrounded by the ubiquitous Celtic crosses.

Back in Slane itself, the Conyngham Arms hotel is a good choice of venue as it is very much in line with the eighteenth Century theme. The 'square', at the intersection at Slane is renowned for the four large Georgian houses known as the four sisters. The Conyngham Arms is a nicely restored eighteenth century coaching Inn, with a front reception and a spacious eating area at the back. The lunch was a little bit on the 'designer' side in terms of portions, but did not break the bank at less than twenty Euros for two courses. The Conyngham Arms fish pie with smoked gubbeen cheese and an herb crust can be recommended. If you were staying over, this is an inexpensive option compared to the rip off prices of the capital, with a double room with breakfast available for less than one hundred Euros.

The Guinness as always is perfectly palatable at the Arms, but if you prefer a pub stop, Dalys bar next door, proved to be an excellent hostelry. The friendly bar staff serve a good pint of the black stuff and the pub appears to have something of a reputation for rock music. Certainly the album covers that adorned the wall in the toilet were an interesting collection from over the years, not least because I seemed to have most of them!

Assessing Scealai Aonair's declining chances. Fairyhouse June 2018.

7

DOWNPATRICK

Downpatrick is one of my favourite courses in Ireland. I was delighted when Shirleys Gold Well was entered by Gordon Elliott to race there on Sunday seventeenth of June. It was a mares' flat race, the last on a jumping card at the quirky, totally unique Northern Irish racecourse.

Gordon considered Shirleys Gold Well a decent prospect. In some respects, she was the potential star of 'our' string. Such optimism had been based on the fact that on her only other start, a year before, she had actually won a point-to-point beating some well regarded types in the process. All 'owners' like to think they have a 'good thing' in the ranks, which is unexposed and can win impressively when they finally run on a course. In the meantime of course, many syndicates use the euphemism, 'they could be anything', to whet the appetites of the members. Gordon was far too wise to be going down that path with a club horse, however he clearly rated the animal and was careful in the way he introduced her to the racecourse.

Optimism was somewhat tempered when she finally made her debut in 'our' colours running in a bumper at Down Royal in March. There were some good horses in that race; in fact Gordon had the favourite, a horse called Tintage that had actually been fourth at the Cheltenham festival the week before. So Shirleys Gold Well was up against it, ran a little green and ended up eighth of the ten runners. Gordon had a 'four timer' at the meeting and Tintage went from last to first in seconds, to win the bumper. Meanwhile, Shirleys Gold Well reappeared a month later at Fairyhouse and appeared not to have 'come on' for her experience at Down Royal, finishing eleventh of the twelve runners. Clearly there was a gap between potential and ability on the racecourse and Shirleys Gold Well was on a steep learning curve. Sensibly Gordon put the horse away for a couple of months as the learning process continued and now hopes were set that she would reappear at Downpatrick and show her real form.

Of course I was fully aware that just because the horse held an entry, this did not mean she would necessarily be declared. I was well versed in this situation from my previous 'owning' experiences and had many times seen a likely run come to nothing. Suffice to say that from my point of view this is a nervous time. However, I had been lucky thus far in seeing 'my' horses run over the water, and I kept everything crossed that Shirleys Gold Well would keep it that way.

Entries cost money and although for this race this would not have been a great deal I took this as a positive while I waited for the declaration announcement.

Forty eight hours before the race I checked on the Horse Racing Ireland web site: there had been twenty one entries for this race, and this had been whittled down to eleven declared horses, Shirleys Gold Well was not amongst them. It is natural to be disappointed when your horse doesn't race and this is doubly the case when the 'shoestring model' has you racing across the Irish Sea. However, this is the nature of racehorse ownership, despite all the best laid plans not all the variables are under your control. Little was forthcoming as to why she didn't race, it would seem that Gordon had decided this was not the race for her. Although I wouldn't now be seeing 'my' horse, I would still go to Downpatrick and see what this unique racecourse had to offer.

RACEDAY – DOWNPATRICK SUNDAY JUNE 17 2018
THE RACECOURSE

The course is located twenty miles south of Belfast, the A7 can get you there quickly, but it's hard to avoid the road congestion in the town centre on race days. Unique is a much over used adjective when it comes to describing racecourses, but in the case of Downpatrick it feels appropriate. It has a distinctly 'local' feel to it, a charming, intimate country course with a quite amazing track for the horses to navigate. Anne Holland in her book, 'Horses for Courses', talks about it being a 'fun fair switchback ride', and this gives a fair indication of what faces horse and jockey. Certain races on this right-handed course start off on the steep finishing straight located in front of the main stand. Once the horses reach the top of this hill, they then descend rapidly away from us and almost disappear from view, before starting on the tough accent up to the highest point on the far side of the course. From there they travel down the hill towards a sharp right hand bend, which leads up to the ridiculously narrow up hill finish (on the second circuit).

In the centre of this vertiginous course stands a working farm where sheep and cattle are spied, along with crops glistening in the afternoon sun. Away to the right of this scene are the majestic mountains of Mourne, which as the song says 'sweep down to the sea'. It's a magical place and today, 'Style Sunday', it's packed to the rafters. The sloping parade ring, neatly squeezed into the area between the jockeys' weighing room and the racetrack, is well populated and the nearby bookies are doing brisk business. There is one main stand, which was built around the millennium, it is able to take today's crowd and affords a good view of the previously described vista. There are tented suites available that seem to be at full capacity, where prosecco and no doubt prawn sandwiches are freely available.

Horses have been racing here for over three hundred years and it hosts the prestigious Ulster National in March. However, it is these summer meetings that might well be the key to the success of country courses in a Country full of racecourses. The programme notes tell me that their attendance figures are increasing year on year and certainly today they are at capacity to see some quality 'jumping' races.

THE RACES

The racing didn't disappoint, with a capacity crowd enjoying some exciting National Hunt racing. Shirleys Gold Well may have been absent, but Gordon was represented in six of the seven races on the card. I decided to follow his horses when my favourite Irish jockey, Davy Russell, rode them. This proved to be a very profitable decision on my part, as Davy came up with a two-timer at inexplicably healthy odds. In both races he showed his expertise at riding this tricky track. Generally he stayed up with the pace throughout and waited to pounce at that critical last bend, scooting up the narrow finishing straight and winning comfortably. To complete a successful punting afternoon my lucky green and red colours came to the fore in the sixth race when Touchedbyanangel romped home at 10/1. It was little wonder I had such positive memories of Downpatrick, as I had backed him half an hour before at 16/1!

WHERE TO STAY AND DRINK THE GUINNESS

If you are heading into Belfast the Crown Bar facing the Opera House is not to be missed. Steeped in tradition, with an ambience characterised by the cosy snugs and brightly coloured tiling, this has claims to be Belfast's premier public house. The Guinness is always top notch and as regards the menu, the Irish stew is suitably filling.

If you are going the other way, across the border to Monaghan, it is worth a trip to the up market Castle Leslie estate, situated at Glaslough. This is an old ascendency house and estate, which has been in the Leslie family for over three hundred years. It made International headlines in 2002 when Paul McCartney and Heather Mills were married in its seventeenth century chapel. With over a thousand acres you could keep with the horsey theme by trying out its equestrian facilities or just go for a ramble through its stunning grounds. The Guinness and food are superb but come at a price. You could stay over, but to do so you would have had to win a lot more money than I managed at Downpatrick!

**A unique course with its 'funfair switchback ride'.
Downpatrick June 2018.**

8

GALWAY

We had left Manchester, known Worldwide as the 'rainy City', after a forty-nine day drought encompassed in the June-July heat wave of 2018, to reach Galway for the summer racing festival, where it was raining! It continued raining off and on from midweek onwards in that characteristic soft mizzle, celebrated in the classic Irish blessing (rains fall soft upon your fields). The north west of Ireland can see off all comers for the title of the rainy capital, this is surely the wettest place in North West Europe.

Of course the weather has an impact on horse racing, affecting the going and determining the opportunities for some of 'my' horses to run. It had been quite a year from a meteorological perspective and this had been a major reason for horses not appearing. In Ireland, Storm Eleanor had struck in January causing extensive flooding, and Storm Emma, bringing snow and ice, in February and March, followed this. The ferocious 'beast from the east', meant racing was restricted in the early spring. Now in high summer we had an extended heat wave with Britain and Ireland receiving sustained high temperatures more familiar to the Mediterranean. The Emerald Isle had turned brown! For Ireland we had now moved into a surreal situation where I was fielding communications that told me runs were unlikely due to the heat or more pertinently, the rock hard ground.

I didn't think it over likely that any of 'my' horses would be good enough to grace the festival, but these extremes in the weather placed question marks over a few horses. On the way over to Galway I had scrutinised press photographs of depleted water levels at nearby Lough Mask and Corrib, which showed the graphic impact of the hot weather. However, as I arrived in the Irish Lake District, it became obvious that these levels were quickly being replenished.

This of course was good news as now it became possible that I might get a runner out west. This had long been the pipe dream as I had researched my family tree that one of 'my' horses would race 'out west'.

Given the quality of the horses attracted to the festival, it seemed excessively optimistic to believe that Galway would be the place where the pipedream became reality. Despite this there had been rumours and indeed an entry for Smiling Eliza to run on the first day of the festival, but this came to nothing. However a more realistic possibility emerged later in the week when it transpired that Gordon was looking at two handicaps at the weekend for Scealai Aonair. It soon became clear that the principal target was a one mile three furlong handicap on the Saturday afternoon, and a firm entry was lodged for this race by midweek.

As we know an entry and a declaration are two very different things, and an entry of sixty-three horses for an eighteen-runner field tempered enthusiasm. Non-the less there were determined soundings from the trainer and I pored over the entries to see if the dream Galway runner was a realistic possibility. Many of these horses had multiple entries at Galway, so that in itself meant they could drop out. The going was now softer than the week before, so maybe that might change the mind of their trainers! One might have been grasping at straws, as the main thing I took from this appraisal was there were many good horses in the entry, a lot of them with a higher BHA mark than Scealai Aonair.

On Friday the third of August I constantly checked the HRI (Horse Racing Ireland) website for the declarations, until at mid day it appeared. I quickly scanned the list of horses and there to my amazement was the name of Scealai Aonair. Unfortunately, next to her name was the word reserve! And to make matters worse she was number twenty-one, which was third reserve. She would now need three of the listed eighteen runners to drop out, if the dream was to be realised. So near and yet so far, it would seem. Despite this in theory I had a runner in the next days racing, indeed the betting sites even gave her a starting price. 16/1 seemed to suggest that she had some sort of chance, but only if she ran.

***

RACEDAY – GALWAY, SATURDAY, AUGUST 4th, 2018
THE RACECOURSE

Galway racecourse is a big course in every sense of the word. The right-handed rectangular course of ten furlongs with a pronounced uphill finish is one of the grandest racecourses in the Country. On race days, the crowds are so large that they appeared to have their own traffic arrangements, as sections of the N5 are coned off, with tunnelled entrances to the extensive car parking lots. Once on the course a wide range of services are available to the public exemplifying the grand scale of operation. If you are feeling in extravagant mood, then you can take the escalator from the main concourse to the Wilson Lynch rooms, where the champagne is quaffed. This is similarly available in the impressive Killanin stand, where the well heeled have their superior views and one presumes food. However, the Millennium main stand is pretty impressive in its own right, with comfortable seating above a terrace, adjacent to the winning post. For the curious, a whole set of buildings stretch out behind the main stand, encompassing the ubiquitous Guinness village, all sorts of food emporiums and a stage where a band were banging out a wholly appropriate version of 'Dirty Old Town'.

The festival is long established in Irish racing history, this would be the 149th Galway races. In the 1960's the festival lasted three days, by the seventies it had extended to five days, this became six in 1982 and a weekly event was established in 1999. It is not just the horses that need to exhibit stamina around here; punters need staying power and long pockets for such an extravaganza. Each day is characterised by high standard races over both flat and jumps, with a feature race worth a very healthy 'pot' to the winner. Its most prestigious feature race is the Galway Plate, always run on the Wednesday of the festival. This is a high quality handicap steeplechase run over two miles six furlongs, with some challenging fences and the steep uphill finish to be negotiated.

Ease of getting around the racecourse can vary greatly depending on which day you visit the festival. The Plate day is actually early evening and on a wet night getting around can be quite a challenge in the hurly burly of a capacity crowd. In many respects the weekend can be the best time to check out the festival, both are day meetings, the Saturday has a business like feel of top class horses going about their business, whereas the Sunday (family day) is by far the most relaxed, with a delightful mix of sprints and distance races over the flat, steeple chasing and hurdle races over the jumps. The parade ring situated away to the right from the tunnelled entrance is like all-else at Galway on a suitably large scale. A stepped approach leads to a wide terrace where the horses can be assessed as they parade around the ring. The tantalising question remained, would I be inside the ring on the Saturday of the festival?

***

PRE RACE

In a Guinness infused sleep on the Friday night I avoided the temptation of wishing for a horsebox pile up on the M6 that led to three early morning withdrawals! I non-the less realised it was going to take a turn of events of this proportion to get my horse in the parade ring for the afternoon race. I maintained a mood of blind optimism right up to the email I received at eleven o clock. Unfortunately it was from the Elliott yard, and it was to tell me that there had been no withdrawals and on that basis Scealai Aonair would not be travelling to Galway on Saturday afternoon. There was natural disappointment at this news. I had never really expected to see 'my' horse at the festival, so in a strange way this process of entry and reserve status, had actually made the news that little bit worse. Still I had the programme for the Saturday race card, with Scealai Aonair printed in bold and I was sure that as the years passed by and the drink had been taken, I'd find that he actually ran that day!

There was something quite poignant about watching the horses parade around the ring for the four ten, McDonogh Capital Investments handicap. The tannoy confirmed that the race card remained unaltered and that the reserves would not run.

***

THE RACES

The race itself was a trappy little flat handicap run over the longer distance of one mile four furlongs. The big stables were well represented but there were the usual dark horses located on lighter weights towards the bottom of the handicap. In the event the winner came from nearer the top of the weights when Share the Honour burst through in the final furlong to snatch victory at 16/1. What was interesting here was that this horse, was owned by a syndicate (like ourselves) and the all-powerful Aiden O'Brien's horse representing the multimillionaires Magnier et al was back in third place. In someway this is the beauty of horse racing, small scale owners with any sense know they are not going to win many races or much money, but they could sometimes have their moment in the sun. I read on my travels that one in every six horses racing in Ireland today is owned by some form of syndicate or race club. Today was not to be for Scealai Aonair, but it was a bumper day for the 'Not Even Maybe' syndicate. As if to emphasise the quixotic nature of events, at least for this week, the multi millionaire horse owner J P McManus had forty-four runners at the festival and only one winner.

Ireland's reserve system had become a major talking point by the end of the week, when it came in for significant criticism in the Racing Post. It wasn't Scealai Aonair's situation that had provoked the comment but the week's big race the Galway Plate. The race was a typically competitive affair with the press and the racing rags selecting nine different winners from the twenty-two runners. The powerhouses of Willie Mullins and Gordon Elliott were well represented with six and four horses respectively. In addition to this were other favoured horses with Harrington, De Broomhead and Fleming. However according to the bookies the night before the race the most talented and potential favourite horse was a listed reserve, Willie Mullins' Patricks Park. The reserve system, like a few other features of racing in Ireland, is somewhat relaxed. Technically a reserve horse could be declared only ninety minutes or less before a race starts. This is exactly what happened on that Wednesday evening, as Patricks Park was declared ninety minutes before the off, with serial winner Ruby Walsh on board. The horse that dropped out due to the going was Ballycasey, a Mullins horse. Given that many punters might well have had their money down by this time, this certainly mixed up the betting market with a new favourite, not a state of affairs that impressed the Racing Post!

In the event, Patricks Park came in a distant second behind Clarcam, a runaway leader that the other horses could not reel in. He saw no other horses as they say to win at 33/1. More tellingly from my perspective, Gordon Elliott trained him! With Gordon it's never enough to think he might win a race like this, the trick is to work out which of his many horses in the race will win. I plumped for Jury Duty with Davy Russell on board; I suppose I should have backed them all!

WHERE TO STAY AND DRINK THE GUINNESS

To avoid the racing crowds of congested Galway we stopped at the tiny village of Clonbur, some forty five kilometres to the north of Galway City. The village lies between Loughs Mask and Corrib in Ireland's 'lake district'. In terms of accommodation the three stars Fairhill hotel is perfectly adequate, offering bed and breakfast at around a 100 Euros a night.

Burke's Bar and Restaurant along the main street is the best stop for Guinness, food and music. It's a traditional pub with the usual long bar and has a cosy restaurant at the rear which serves good meat and fish dishes, often accompanied by their home baked soda bread. There has long been a debate about the correct temperature at which to serve Guinness. The more flavoursome drink and the one I remember best was always served at room temperature. Many years ago the landlord of this pub emphasised the quality of this drink against the encroaching 'cold' Guinness movement that was clearly being aimed at a younger lager drinking public. Tomas Burke and Leo Moran made the news headlines, when the Saw Doctors lead guitarist demanded the 'warm Guinness' These days that debate is lost and all Guinness seems to be served at a cool 6 degrees, but at least this wasn't the dreaded 'extra cold' drink and it went down well.

As a break from the frenetic pace of the Galway festival, visit the charming, tourist village of Cong, some eight kilometres away. Cong was the location for John Ford's famous 1952 film, 'The Quiet Man'. With its breathtaking early techni color sets and lush, romantic view of the 'old country', some see the film as the legendary director's 'love letter' to Ireland. Over time some have come to the conclusion that in fact it was Hollywood hokum, as the Urban dictionary might have it; a classic slice of Paddywackery, 'fakey out of a box Irishness'. There is even some horse racing in the film, when John Wayne directed the scenes of beach racing, during Ford's illness. What ever your view of the film, it seems to have been a Godsend to Cong both in the 1950s and today when over fifty thousand tourists come each year to see the place where the film was shot.

The finishing straight, first circuit on the 'quiet Sunday'. Notice Ballybrit castle in the background. Galway August 2018.

9

ROSCOMMON

I moved onto Roscommon hoping it would be second time lucky in my quest to have a runner in the west. Two consecutive entry and non-declarations at Down Patrick and Galway had emphasised what a difficult task it was to get 'your' horse to the races. Non-the less I remained bullish about my chances as there had been a raft of entries for early August and amongst them were two live chances for a meeting at Roscommon. As a further bonus this meeting was my favoured National Hunt code, so I took this as a good omen.

Smiling Eliza was one of the two horses entered at Roscommon. She of course was one of 'our' string's winners and I had seen her run a good race at Fairyhouse. She had followed this race up with a great effort at the Curragh on the Irish Derby weekend, coming in third and confirming that she was the best horse in 'our' string. The really exciting news, from my perspective, was that Gordon had decided to see what she was like over hurdles. She had been schooled over the previous couple of weeks and had apparently made a good impression. As usual though there were doubts over her participation as I noted that she had also been entered at other racecourses in the same week.

Crack of Thunder was the other horse with an entry at Roscommon. He was another new horse to 'our' string and he was an imposing looking steeplechaser. This was all very exciting, as there is little to compare with a steeplechaser taking on those bigger fences and hopefully galloping away to victory over a three-mile track. He had come from England where he would appear to have done very little for trainer Charlie Longsden. However, he did have some point-to-point form, having won a couple of contests. At the end of July, Gordon had sent him off for a debut run at Perth, where the champion jockey Richard Johnson did the steering. I watched the race on my computer and a very strange story unfolded.

Because Gordon has such a good record at Perth virtually every horse he saddles vies for favouritism. This is particularly the case when the champion jockey is on board and this occasion was no different as 'our' horse was evens favourite. However, I found this state of affairs hard to fathom, the horse hadn't run for fourteen months and although Gordon is a top trainer, he had only had the horse for a short time. I put my money down with little conviction and the horse duly ran a most underwhelming race, finishing fifth of nine. Clearly 'in need of the race', word filtered through that the horse finished strongly and Gordon was firmly of the opinion that he would do better over a longer distance.

This news worked very much in my favour, as there were not too many three-mile chases on the calendar at that time, and the Roscommon race became a serious possibility. I checked out the entries and was further encouraged by the fact that only twenty-two horses had entered the race and a maximum of sixteen were permitted to compete. I was now seriously optimistic and waited for the email that might confirm my expectations. Early on Monday August sixth the news came through: not only was Crack of Thunder declared for the three mile chase but Smiling Eliza was going to make her hurdles debut. After all the recent frustrations, this was brilliant news. Smiling Eliza's schooling had gone well and Denis O'Regan would ride and I was made up when I heard that my favourite Irish jockey Davy Russell would partner Crack of Thunder. It would seem that whenever I was destined to see 'my' horses run, they would come two by two!

***

RACE DAY – CRACK OF THUNDER and SMILING ELIZA AT ROSCOMMON
TUESDAY, AUGUST 7, 2018
THE RACECOURSE

Roscommon is a typical Country course, located eighty miles west of Dublin. Some one of a pernickety persuasion might even question whether it was in the 'west', but Roscommon is one of the five Counties in Ireland's most westerly province, Connacht. I was back in the owner's facility today and if truth be told they were a little rudimentary in comparison with the Curragh, but non the less a welcome start to the evening's racing. The owners and trainers facility was located in a portacabin, close to the casualty unit, which unfortunately was to come into play later in the evening. The tea and coffee was in abundant supply, but you had to pay for your biscuits!

There appeared to be one main grandstand, laid out in traditional terrace fashion. It had an owner's section adjacent to the winning post, but I eschewed that for a central location that offered fine views of the course and the large television screen. If you want a drink, a snack or the tote they are readily available on a large concourse under the stand or in a cosier lounge on the top of the stand.

Racing here goes back to the 1830s, when it was organised by the British who had a garrison based here. This is one of Ireland's summer racecourses, with nine meetings planned between May and September. There are a couple of tight bends on the course but they have a long galloping stretch in between. With this being the first jumps meeting that one of 'my' horses had raced in, I went to have a closer look at the obstacles. While they were not Aintree they might be a test for a young horse making her hurdling debut or for a steeplechaser who hadn't seen many of the larger obstacles over the last twelve months.

***

PRE RACE

Pre race activity in the parade ring can be a surreal experience. Roscommon parade ring on the evening of Tuesday the seventh of August was a perfect example of this. As usual the relaxed ring procedure meant that nobody seemed particularly bothered about checking my badge as I entered the quirky sloping parade ring.

On this occasion, even though Crack of Thunder was out already and strutting his stuff it was hard to identify my fellow 'owners' in the ring. Usually wherever the crowd is congregated would be a safe bet to be the Elliott 'owners', but it would seem not so many of them had ventured west. Things were not made any clearer by the fact that Gordon had still not arrived as Davy Russell appeared from the weighing room. Davy seemed equally lost as he attempted to locate the 'owners' and we all literally bumped into each other in the centre of the ring. There were about six of us that crowded around the champion jockey. It is of course a somewhat superficial experience, as we are all strangers to one another and only have the horse in common. Initially it would appear that we were in awe of the great man as very little was said as we stood staring at each other. Davy finally broke the impasse by murmuring something about the weather and questioning whether the rain would keep away.

Usually in this situation there are questions about tactics or how the course is riding, but somehow all this seemed superfluous. Davy was in the zone, concentrating no doubt about the dubious privilege of steering Crack of Thunder over the larger obstacles. Jump jockeys have a tough job, attempting to keep horse and body intact whilst tackling the larger obstacles; it is not a walk in the park. Davy was clearly concentrating on the job in hand and I for one was not going to ask some damn fool questions about the going!

At this point Gordon appeared, cheery and outgoing, he shook hands and quickly gave his assessment of 'our' horse. This was a big horse that would go better in a winter slog and tonight's run was over a longer distance, which Gordon thought might suit. The general drift appeared to be that a place might be a good result and that the race was a learning experience, for all concerned. This was an interesting exchange, as it hadn't escaped my attention that our horse was the short price favourite and he was certainly not drifting in the market (losing favouritism). Still I suppose Gordon doesn't set the odds, but I decided to reduce my betting stake somewhat and like all the others, see what happened.

***

THE RACE - HANDICAP STEEPLECHASE, 3 MILES 124 Yards

With three circuits of the racecourse to run, over three miles and taking on fifteen fences this was going to be a test of stamina. Nobody told the veteran horse Old Supporter, who bolted away at the start and had soon built up a significant lead. Crack of Thunder's jumping appeared clean if somewhat deliberate, and he seemed to be moving freely enough as he settled in with the chasing pack in fifth position.

After one circuit he maintained his position and although he was jumping the fences slightly to his left, he appeared to be going well enough. As he reached the half way stage, he seemed to be in a steady rhythm and I wondered if Davy might be biding his time, before making his move in the latter part of the race. However, by the end of the second circuit, his progress did not seem so smooth, as he was passed by horses and drifted back to tenth place. As the third circuit unfolded, Davy appeared to be steadying his mount; the horse maintained his midfield position and all the horses approached the back straight fences. Coming to the last fence in the back straight they were bunched together and I could only just make out Davy's black hat, as the horses took the obstacle together. I didn't see the hat again, because as the horses came down on the other side and moved away from the fence, I could make out the figures of horse and jockey splayed out on the turf. The tannoy, relayed the news instantly, Crack of Thunder had fallen!

I kept the binoculars trained on the area, where thankfully Crack of Thunder got up from the ground and chased after the other horses, but Davy remained grounded. Initially on his haunches, he attempted to get up, but soon subsided to the ground in obvious pain. Ringstone Castle eventually caught Old Supporter, to win the race at 16/1.

***

POST RACE

Gordon had waited patiently on the edge of the course, clearly hoping that his injured jockey would recover. However, the last sight we had was of ambulances and stretchers being employed as Davy was transported away from the fence and was in fact on his way to hospital. A couple of the 'owners' came together, one commenting that it was never a good sight to see stretchers, another retorting that these days it was mandatory. However, before the start of the next race it was announced that Davy Russell had been stood down for the rest of the night, so clearly his injuries had necessitated the hospital visit. No specific news was forthcoming on the course that night, but later in the evening the Racing Post reported: 'Champion jockey in leg injury following fall'. At the bottom of the piece the report quoted the Tullamore hospital as saying he had sustained a tibia fracture. This was indeed a dramatic dénouement to 'my' first jumper on the Irish journey, although the news was better the next day, when Russell reported the injury to be mere bruising. Tough men, these jockeys.

Within the hour we were preparing for 'our' second runner and hoping for better luck.

***

PRE RACE

This time being more familiar with each other, we had no problem meeting in the centre of the parade ring. Gordon had another horse running in this race, the red-hot favourite Elysian Plains, whose owners held a more exalted position than us, as they were the Gigginstown Stud. Due to Davy Russell's unfortunate injury, Gordon had hurriedly arranged for crack jockey Barry Geraghty to ride this horse and he initially went over to him to discuss tactics. We gathered around our jockey the experienced Denis O'Regan, who seemed very cheery and upbeat as he shook every ones hand. He seemed well briefed on 'our' horse and said he would try to keep him 'handy' and see where he was at the business end of the race.

Gordon finally made his way over and quickly reaffirmed he liked Smiling Eliza, a good horse that had run well in the past and he seemed genuinely hopeful he could run well tonight. This was a juvenile hurdle race and of course it was Smiling Eliza's first attempt over hurdles, so a lot was going to have to be taken on trust. Given what had just happened to Davy Russell, there was even more sincerity in our parting words to Denis, 'to come back safe'. Certainly Smiling Eliza looked sharp and up for business as she departed the parade ring, but the markets were hardening on Elysian Plain, napped (tipped to win) in the programme and now trading at 6/4 on.

***

THE RACE – MAIDEN HURDLE, 2 MILES 96 Yards

Smiling Eliza quickly settled into a smooth rhythm and was up with the front-runners as she smoothly hurdled her first obstacle. They were going at quite a clip and soon a group of five horses with Elysian Plain prominent broke away from the other horses. Smiling Eliza trailed in the second group, but she seemed to be going well enough, jumping the hurdles in an accomplished manner.

With just under a mile left, Elysian Plain made his move and moved into the lead with Parisian in close pursuit. Smiling Eliza remained in touch and in fact began to make stealthy progress through the chasing pack.

As they reached the top of the course and turned towards the finishing straight Elysian Plain maintained his lead, but Smiling Eliza was making unmistakeable progress, closing the gap to a couple of lengths and now racing in third place. As the horses jumped the third last a visibly tiring Elysian Plain succumbed to Parisian and now it was Smiling Eliza going really well, who set after the new leader. There was only a length between the horses as they approached the final fence and I began to dream that this could be the moment, a winner in the West! Certainly to the naked eye Smiling Eliza was going the better of the two and Parisian's jockey had to work hard to maintain his lead.

Alas it was not to be, Parisian toughed it out and although Smiling Eliza tantalisingly began to close the gap, the line came too soon and 'our' valiant horse finished in second place.

***

POST RACE

I quickly made my way back to the parade ring, where a couple of 'owners' were crowding around Denis and Gordon, who were stood next to the second place post. Denis was giving a very upbeat debrief and was full of praise for Smiling Eliza. She had given him a good ride all the way round, he ventured, and when he had asked her to quicken she responded straight away. She's a good 'un was the clear message and it will not be long until she wins. We congratulated Denis on a stylish ride and with that he tipped his cap and was gone. Gordon, who might have had mixed feelings, after all we had beaten the hot favourite, was clearly impressed with the horse's efforts. For her first time over hurdles it was a great run, in his opinion, and he was sure there was more to come. With that we all shook hands and wished Gordon the best of luck for what was already proving to be an eventful night.

Smiling Eliza had departed the scene, but she had maintained her position as 'our' top horse and had come so close to providing me with that elusive Irish winner, in a night of high drama.

WHERE TO STAY AND DRINK THE GUINNESS

Thinking that Scealai Aonair might run at Sligo, we had pitched up at the north-western City and that is where we remained for the racing at Roscommon. Sligo is one of my favourite places in Ireland, a beguiling mix of coastal scenery and literary heritage. Travel to Drumcliffe, north of the centre to WB Yeats grave with its famous epitaph 'Cast a cold eye on life, on death. Horseman pass by!' If you wanted to immerse yourself in Yeats you could travel out to see the site of one of his most famous works; 'The Lake Isle of Innisfree'. You can find this haunting spot to the south east of the centre, on Lough Gill.

While you are at Drumcliffe call in at the Yeats Tavern. This is a large-scale hostelry that serves excellent Guinness and the food is of restaurant quality.

In terms of accommodation we stayed at the relatively new motel style Red Cottage and Stables. This is a very impressive B&B run by a young and enterprising couple, Tomas and Karen. To keep with the equine theme, we stayed in the converted former stables. These have been very tastefully modernised with all mod cons and are certainly comparable with hotel fixtures and fittings. An imaginative breakfast menu means that the place comes highly recommended.

'We were that close'... Denis O'Regan seems to be saying in his debrief, myself and Gordon Elliott to his right.

Roscommon August 2018.

10

BALLINROBE

Buoyed with the dramatic events at Roscommon I was a satisfied man, I had my runner 'out west' and came so close to that elusive winner. It was something of a surprise therefore when I received news that I had another potential runner at Ballinrobe. This was particularly exciting news, as Ballinrobe was Mayo's only racecourse and this meant I may have a runner in the County of my parents' birth.

This good news was tempered somewhat by the fact that the potential runner was Scealai Aonair. Scealai in recent weeks had become my 'nearly' horse, having come tantalisingly close to giving me a Galway festival runner and also having an entry at Sligo, which she didn't take up. So consequently although I was delighted with the possibility of a runner at Ballinrobe, I remained somewhat circumspect.

Scealai Aonair of course had been 'our' winner at Clonmel and had run when I attended Fairyhouse. Although that day she was up against it and showed little, there was a feeling that she was a decent flat horse and that in a less demanding race she may well return to the winner's enclosure. Ballinrobe appeared on the surface, to be just that opportunity. The race, the last on the card on Monday thirteenth of August, was a fairly modest looking handicap run over a distance of one mile five furlongs. The race was open to horses that had a handicap mark of between forty-five and sixty-five. Scealai Aonair was one of the higher rated horses at a mark of sixty-one, but the rather off putting news was, there were over fifty entries for a race with a maximum field of fourteen horses.

Gordon wasn't giving much away, but the overall news from the stables was that the horse was well and could be ready for another run. The slightly worrying caveat was that it might depend on the weight that Scealai Aonair was allocated. Non the less I dutifully checked through all the entries and kept everything crossed as I waited for any news of a declaration. All Friday passed without any news and given the proximity of the race date I took this as a somewhat ominous silence. However, when I checked the Irish Racehorse web site I noted that although the weekend was now upon us, the race was at the same stage and in fact none of the horses had been declared yet.

The declarations finally appeared on the Monday morning and I quickly scanned the fourteen horses, only to find that Scealai Aonair was not amongst them. This was disappointing if not unsurprising news and just as I was about to close the screen I noticed that suddenly an eighth race had appeared on the card. What had happened was the final race had been split and now there were another fourteen horses that had been declared to run. Maybe fate had one final trick in store for me and I quickly reopened the list of horses to see if Scealai was amongst them. The sense of reprieve did not last long, as once again her name was absent and in a perverse way this made the disappointment all the greater.

As I had found on my trip around Ireland, there were no guarantees when it came to getting your horse to the races. With or without the horse I would endeavour to enjoy the Ballinrobe races. As a further treat to my horseracing odyssey around Ireland, I had a long-term arrangement to meet my sister Elaine and her husband Joel at the meeting. It seemed very appropriate to meet Elaine at Mayo's only racecourse, as although she lives in Cape Cod in America, she is my families 'Irish' representative having had a house in Mayo for over twenty-five years.

THE RACECOURSE

Ballinrobe is a classic Country course and on this sunlit night was looking at its best. Racing has a long tradition here going back to 1774 and at this venue, since 1921. In 2018 it had a fixture list of ten meetings, with nearly all of them run in the twilight slot between five and nine pm. The meets are run between April and September to maximise its attraction to locals and holidaymakers alike.

It is located about a mile outside of town and is found in a natural amphitheatre that gives a fantastic view of the entire course. This is a rural, not to say rustic environment, with Lough Corrib in the near distance and the Partry Mountains looking down on proceedings. It is a right-handed course, with an undulating backstretch and a fairly gentle right-handed bend to the home straight. Both Flat and National Hunt racing occurs here, although tonight's card would be contested on the level.

Ballinrobe's rustic charm belies a range of facilities, which are first class. Apparently the course won an award for best racecourse in Ireland in 2012, and looking around me I could see why. There was a good crowd of around two and a half thousand gathered in warm sunshine and they appeared well catered for. The Corrib restaurant is a large airy eatery and if you want the more up market option the Corranna restaurant was open for bookings. The Mask pavilion under the main stand is the usual combination of bars, cafes and tote facilities. My attention was drawn to the multitude of photographs that adorn the walls; these serve as a kind of unofficial history of Mayo's only racecourse. There is a picture of the local equine hero, Dorans Pride, who made his debut here and went on to great things both in Ireland and Cheltenham. However, my attention was drawn to the picture of the legendary English jockey, Lester Piggott. To be honest, I was surprised to see the iconic figure, of English flat racing, so far out West. It would appear that in his second coming, as a jockey of some fifty-five years of age, he drew the capacity crowd of five thousand here in 1991; needless to say he had a winner.

The far end of the racecourse contains a very impressive modern jockey weighing room and a fairly large, beautifully manicured parade ring. There would be no need to visit it tonight, but the race cards looked interesting. My American brother in law had an individual approach to the evening's racing, as he had decided on just one bet for the night, and was waiting for the last race, where he had selected a horse called US Navy Seal. I couldn't be certain whether this reflected some inside knowledge on his part and therefore would involve a massive punt or if he just liked the name! We made our way to the impressive main grandstand, a large terraced affair, with a row of seating at the very top, and looked forward to a good evening's racing and maybe some winners to compensate for my absent horse.

THE RACES

The first races were tricky affairs with few winners to be had, although my sister did manage one in the third race, and she felt this might set her up for the night. With Joel's 'certainty' to come later on in the evening, we looked forward with some anticipation to race four, due to go 'off' at 6.20 pm.

Watching horses in the parade ring is one of the honoured practices of going racing, where the better-informed racegoer can glean a lot in determining their final selection. Is the horse well turned out? Does it appear to be on 'its toes'? Has it got a sparkle in its eye? Or does it appear to be a walking mirage of a black hole, a repository of your disappearing Euros? For this race I had plumped for number nine on the card, the apparent no hoper; Alpine Pass. During the parade, I had noticed that the horse's number on the saddle had slipped and so momentarily it looked as though there were two number six horses in the race. This I convinced myself was a sign from above, desperation had clearly taken hold following my recent barren punting run. Still it couldn't do any worse than my first three selections for the night and so with such meticulous analysis completed, I went to place my bet and make my way to the Grandstand.

Once I was in place I was facing a large television screen, which showed the horses still parading, and a list of the latest odds. I suppose the first indication I had that things were not as normal was when I looked at my watch which showed it was six twenty, but the horses were still in the parade ring and their jockeys were no where to be seen. I kept my eyes on the screen for the next few minutes, as it now resembled one of those television sitcoms, which appear to be on a permanent time loop. Round and round went the horses, with still no sign of any action. Now eight minutes past the 'off' the horses maintained the circulatory movement, but from what I could detect the crowd didn't appear to be in the slightest concerned. Of course this is Ireland I thought, things are very relaxed and laid back here and no doubt there is a reason for a delay, which only appeared to be concerning myself. After eleven minutes and with the first signs of some disquiet from the crowd, the tannoy cranked into action announcing curtly that racing had been abandoned for the night!

The announcement further added that the decision had been taken in the 'interests of track safety'. The interminable delay had apparently been caused by a delegation of jockeys to the stewards' room, where they had voiced their concerns about the safety of the ground. The stewards had deliberated with them and the trainers and had subsequently decided to abandon the meeting. The assembled crowd took this sensational news that would probably have caused a riot at Haydock, on a Saturday afternoon, with calm deliberation. Long queues now snaked back from the tote windows as the punters claimed their money back and even longer queues formed in the car park as people made for the exit.

The 'shoestring' story was ending in the deepest of irony. Ireland, a Country whose greenness gives testimony to its plentiful rainfall supply was suffering because of the summer's heat wave. The excessive heat it would appear had made the ground a little friable, this had meant that it was 'quick' underneath and the jockeys felt that the ground was shifting beneath them. Clearly this was unsafe for horse and jockey and was the reason for the cancellation.

In a greater irony still, I stared at the void races, seven and eight and thought of all those anxious days waiting for Scealai Aonair to be declared. Ballinrobe had been the ultimate example of how difficult it could be to get your horse to the races! In a perverse way I now felt so much better about Scealai Aonair's absence, I am sure I wouldn't have been so sanguine about the way the night turned out if Scealai had been on the card!

WHERE TO STAY AND DRINK THE GUINNESS

We were based some eighteen miles north of Ballinrobe at the pretty and touristy town of Westport. There is no shortage of bars along the triangular shaped centre based around the impressive statue of St Patrick. Matt Molloy's of Chieftans fame draws the crowds, but my own favourite is the more authentic McCarthy's traditional bar. The Guinness is top notch and quickly has you in the mood for some di didli.

In terms of accommodation the Westport Coast Hotel is the four star option, I have stayed here before and it is perfectly acceptable with a pleasant bar and lounge area. However, its restaurant is their main attraction with the menu and service first class. For a more intimate and homely experience I would recommend a stop with Dave at the Quay West. Here the quintessentially charming host dispenses good advice and bonhomie in equal measure.

For those of a more energetic nature attempt to climb Croagh Patrick, located some five miles outside Westport. This is Ireland's holy mountain and at over two thousand five hundred feet its conical shape can be seen from all around Westport. It cannot however be seen at all times, as often it is covered in cloud and rain! So great care must be taken when attempting to climb the rock strewn treacherous accent. It's worth it though as the view (on a clear day) from the top of Clew Bay below is quite spectacular.

Given the equine theme of this book, for those of an historical persuasion it is worth taking a trip out to Carnacon. There you will find the ghostly façade of Moore Hall, on Muckloon hill overlooking Lough Carra. The old ascendency houses of Ireland are often associated with overbearing aristocratic landlords living the good life while the local populace starved. Moore Hall couldn't be further from that image, with George Henry Moore lionised in the famine years as a champion of famine relief and the proud boast was that none of his tenants died in the great hunger. Moore was also a brilliant horseman; he rode Tinderbox in the 1845 Grand National and his own horse Coramma to victory in the Chester Cup a year later. The story goes that his winnings offset by betting against his own horses, produced the funds that helped to feed his tenants. Ironically seventy years later in the midst of the Irish civil war, the anti treaty forces burnt Moore Hall down, leaving the façade we see today. If you take a walk in the grounds you will see a plaque that makes amends for the misguided arson attack praising the Moore family for their famine relief.

With Sue, but no horse and no races! Ballinrobe August 2018.

11

WAY OUT WEST

In terms of a Football analogy, I have always thought of the Irish as the Brazilians of horse racing! It would seem to me that there is a love of horses that comes as easily to the Irish as political debate. The breeding and racing of horses has for hundreds of years been a hobby and a livelihood for many of them. It sometimes appears that virtually all the jockeys in racing are Irish and a high proportion of the top trainers too. Indeed if you were going back in time towards the starting point of recorded Irish history and examined the Book of Kells you would find horses featured amongst the illustrations.

Most people are aware that steeple chasing, that staple of the English racing calendar, has its origins in the Emerald Isle. This relates to the famous match in 1752 between Mr Blake and Mr O'Callaghan, when their horses raced between Buttevant church in County Cork and the spire of St Leger church. The steeples were used as markers for their visibility, as the race was run over four and a half miles in open country.

Horse ownership, training and racing was the preserve of the land owning classes. These people were almost exclusively part of the ascendency elite that had such close ties with the English colonial settlers. John Welcome talks of the first races on the hallowed Curragh being run solely for the 'nobility and gentry'. It is noticeable how horse racing appeared to be immune from the ravages of Ireland's tortured history. Trace the chronology of some of Ireland's great race meetings and take note of how few interruptions were caused by pestilence or war. The seismic events of the great famine appeared to have little impact on these gentlemen's sport, as John Welcome puts it; 'the famine scarcely touched upon the rich and the landed, save in some cases to make their rents less secure'. Easter 1916 is a fateful moment in Irish history, but the Irish Grand National still took place, with a horse called All Sorts victorious.

This is not to say that the Irish were not capable of giving the English a run for their money in equine matters, indeed by the nineteenth Century a trend was set that in some ways led to the relative dominance that the Irish would enjoy by the early twenty first Century. The story in very broad terms sees Irish horse racing going from the deeds of the plucky underdog to the omnipotence of the billionaire Irish stud operations. Such a journey initially had to overcome deeply in grained English prejudice; Chris McGrath quotes a mid nineteenth Century view of the merits of the Irish as, 'when we compare the few ragged, half stud, half potato farms over there, with the many princely establishments amongst us'.

For many a starting point in a gradual change of perception might have come with the famous tale of the Paddereen mare in the 1740s. This involved a Curragh Plate winner Irish Lass and her contest with the aristocratic Sir Ralph Gore's horse Black and All Black. With the nobility supporting the English favourite, the story goes that Irish Lass's owner Mr Archibald tied a Paidrin (Gaelic for Rosary) around his horse's neck, to in John Welcome's memorable phrase, 'place not only his money, but his prayers' on the mare. Needless to say, the Irish horse won, the West was awake!

Perceptions were changed totally by the advent of Ireland's first thoroughbred, Birdcatcher, in the 1830s. The horse was a seriously quick animal, but confined his entire racing career to the Curragh, so in that sense did not seem to immediately change the proper order. It was however, his performance at stud that propelled Irish racing to the very forefront of equine breeding, as he became one of the most successful stallions of all time. Almost immediately his progeny had an impact across the Irish Sea, he sired seven classic winners, with most notably Daniel O'Rourke winning the Derby and The Baron, the St Ledger. This was a revolutionary turn of events, Christopher McGrath sums up his ground breaking impact thus; 'he raced under the aegis of Anglo-Irish landlords, who supervised the Turf of Ireland as ruthlessly as the rest of her soil, but the fact remains that both his parents were born and raced here, and he would in turn sire a son to propagate the genius of Irish horsemanship'. The 'son' was The Baron and he set a higher standard still as he won major races and record purses, as a precocious three year old, over the water. The genetic linkage was established and went from strength to strength, as John Welcome summarises; ' The Baron got Stockwell 'emperor of stallions'; Stockwell got Doncaster and Bend Or, both Derby winners; and Bend Or sired Ormonde, one of the greatest racehorses of all time'.

Ninety five percent of all thoroughbreds are descended from the Darley Arabian horse and Birdcatcher's line could be traced back to this dominant horse. Birdcatcher made his own imprint on that Arabian legacy, as Chris McGrath points out; 'even today silver flecks in the root of a horse's tail, or sprinkled over its flanks, are known as 'birdcatcher ticks''. From this moment onwards the Irish had established themselves as John Welcome puts it; 'they had demonstrated to the World that Irish breeding and Irish racehorses could hold their own anywhere'. As the twentieth Century unfolded, the story continued its upward trajectory.

It is not the aim of this book to write a history of racing in Ireland, far greater tomes than this one, can manage that task. However, in the context of my own horse racing adventures it is pertinent to highlight some horses and individuals in modern times that have elevated the Irish to a position of pre eminence. Orby's victory in the Derby of 1907 was one such moment. Owned by 'Boss' Croker of Tammany Hall fame and trained by another Mr McCabe, this horse became the first Irish trained horse to win English Flat racing's blue ribbon event. John Welcome illustrated the significance of this achievement, when he recalled the old Ladies famous response as McCabe led the horse back into the ring; ' Thank God, and you sir, we have lived to see a Catholic horse win the Derby!' The fact they had to wait another fifty-one years for the second horse to achieve this, tells us the Irish accent was a gradual one.

Vincent O'Brien's phenomenal achievements after the second World War put such statistics in context and established training feats not reached on either side of the Irish Sea. Initially his successes were confined to National Hunt racing. Already successful in his native land, he began to plunder the big prizes over the water and in so doing, established himself at the forefront of National Hunt racing. His horse Cottage Rake started the process in 1948 winning the prestigious Cheltenham Gold Cup. He then proceeded to win it for the next two years with the same horse; Cottage Rake became only the third horse in the history of the race (to this point) to have won it more than once. By 1953 the trainer further burnished his gilded reputation by winning the Gold Cup (with Knock Hard) and the English Grand National (with, Early Mist), in the same year. His appetite in this code was not sated yet and he proceeded to win the next two Nationals with Royal Tan and Quare Times, becoming the first trainer to achieve this hatrick.

It is hard to believe but the maestro achieved even greater accomplishments once he turned his attentions to British flat racing. Without taking into account all his many triumphs on the flat, his achievements just in the English Derby alone, are instructive in terms of how this man raised the status of Irish horse racing to the very pinnacle of the sport. In 1962 his horse Larkspur became only the third Irish trained winner of the famous race and yet over the next twenty years, he would win it five more times. Some of these five winners were arguably amongst flat racings' greatest names, including: Sir Ivor, Nijinsky, Roberto, The Minstral, and Golden Fleece. The scale of O'Brien's groundbreaking achievements was perhaps best exemplified by Nijinsky's performance in 1970 when he won the triple crown of the two thousand Guineas, the Derby and the St. Ledger. Because these premier flat races are run over different distances, it would take a remarkable horse and trainer to achieve such a feat. When Vincent O'Brien achieved this it was the first time it had been done for thirty-five years, it has never been achieved subsequently.

If any horse has ever transcended the sport, it is almost certainly the Irish steeplechaser, Arkle. 'Himself' was as likely to be on the front page as the sporting pages of newspapers in the early 1960s. The bare statistics are of an equine champion who won twenty two of the twenty six races he competed in, recording three successive Gold Cup victories, a couple of Hennessy's and a Whitbred Cup. Of course these were victories achieved on English turf and in line with went before the crux of the story were his dramatic battles with the supposedly unbeatable English Champion, Mill House. His victories in these contests established his immortal reputation in jumping history. Arkle though had a wider appeal; he caught the public imagination and spawned an equine celebrity market, ahead of its time. At home in Manchester, we even called our cat after him! If you visit the Irish National Stud, you can see a full-scale skeleton of the great horse, a permanent reminder of his iconic status. Robin Oakley, in his book, 'The top 100 racehorses of all time', was fulsome in his praise, and placed 'himself', the greatest racehorse of all time.

In modern times, Aiden O'Brien (no relation) has maintained Vincent O'Brien's standards on the flat. Training for the dominant Irish Coolmore operation based at Ballydoyle in Tipperary, their success is a reflection of the ongoing dominance of the Irish thoroughbred horse. Once more the list of their success is far too long to outline here, but it is instructive to touch upon a couple of these outstanding horses' achievements to understand the scale of success. At the start of the Twenty First century Galileo, won six times in just eight races, including victories in both the English and Irish derbies. More significantly, this horse whose breeding goes all the way back to the Darley Arabian, had now become the leading sire in the World of horse racing. Another champion Yeats, reeled off four consecutive Ascot Gold Cups. O'Brien himself has continued to break all records, winning three consecutive Derbies with Camelot, Ruler of The World and Australia. A final example of the remarkable accent of Irish racing was the trainer's exceptional performance in 2017, when he recorded a World record twenty-six group one victories in the calendar year.

Not that the National Hunt sphere should be overlooked, as the new Century saw sterling achievements over the jumps. Willie Mullins was chiefly responsible for this success, becoming annually one of the top trainers at jumping's most prestigious event; the Cheltenham festival. Famously his horse Quevega won the mares hurdle a record six times and in 2015 he set a new record when winning eight times at the festival. As this book has illustrated Gordon Elliott is now reaching the same lofty heights and as a reflection of this in 2018 he equalled Mullins record by achieving eight victories at the Cheltenham festival. In conclusion it would be fair to say that the increased perception of Irish racing brought about by Birdcatcher, has more than been matched by the subsequent achievements of Irish horse, breeding, training and jockeys.

Obviously 'my' horses were far from the blue bloods outlined in the paragraphs above, but I was more than happy with the results of my 'shoestring ownership'. I had set out to see, if I could manage a runner or two back in Ireland and given the speculative nature of the venture, I had to be pleased with the outcome. To 'own' an eyelash on the six million guinea horse, Marsha, and to be in the 'ring' with her at one of the World's most famous racecourses, was the stuff of dreams. Ironically the fact that this odds on 'certainty', didn't actually win the race, mattered little in retrospect. Similarly for one of 'my' horses to bring me to the home of the Irish Grand National, was deeply satisfying. Finally to follow my horses out west, to the province of Connacht from where my family had originated, was the ultimate achievement and vindication of my long-term plan. The fact that a couple of horses ran there and indeed one very nearly won was the proverbial icing on the cake. The 'shoestring' journey proved just how difficult it could be to actually get 'your' horse to the races. However, all those frustrations were accepted as part of the 'game' and made the appearance of six horses at four different courses all the more satisfying. As Stan Hey, whose book unwittingly motivated this trilogy, memorably stated, 'that owners developed an innate sense of the value they are getting from their involvement with horses, one that doesn't involve prize money or winnings from bets'. The Irish adventure certainly bore this out, it could be summarised in his terms as a 'triumph of optimism over cynicism'.

While I was in the west, my mind went back to the Cawley and Carey families that I had studied while researching my family tree. The principal players are of course not with us now, but I revisited the cemeteries where they were laid to rest. The small cemetery at Ballinhaglish, just a few miles south of Ballina is where I found the gravestone of my Grandparents, William and Mary Cawley. There is a prominent Celtic cross, erected at some expense I would have thought by their daughter Evelyn. I wandered around the cemetery and found Mary, Jackie and Mickey Walsh, bringing back memories of those summer holidays of many years ago. In the far corner of the graveyard was a stone for Tom Cawley. There was sense of symmetry that in the year of my project, the last of the Cawley, Carey siblings, had died at the grand old age of ninety-four.

The only Grandparent who was alive when I was born and whom I met was my Mother's Mother, Bridget. Nan as she was known, must have been some woman. Widowed at the age of forty-four, with eight children to raise and with economic prospects limited in one of the poorest corners of Ireland, her survival and achievement was remarkable. I remember her when I was a kid on holiday at the old farm, she was dressed from tip to toe in all black, with a stick helping her as her eyesight was failing and she was a great dispenser of giant mints.

I visited the town of Bangor Erris, and if truth were told it didn't seem very different, to how I had remembered it as a boy. This has been a remote part of Ireland, hard to cultivate and equally hard to make a decent living from. However, in the modern Ireland, it has been discovered by the tourist industry and its rugged topography and pretty beaches now forms part of the Wild Atlantic Way. I went out to the cemetery just outside of Bangor Erris and had no trouble finding Bridget and Anthony's gravestone. There is some doubt that Anthony is actually in this plot as he died so many years before, but his name is marked onto the white gravestone next to the wife he pre deceased by forty two years. Looking around the smart well-kept graveyard, I found the graves of Hugh and Sarah, the brother and sister of my mother and the ones that stayed out west.

Life's circumstances and the economic situation had forced my mother to leave Bangor Erris and never return in a permanent capacity. But my mother always returned and retained her love of the west, and subtly reinforced this message to her children. I went out to the lonely but quite beautiful strand at Doolough, Nan was born here just a quarter of a century after hundreds of famine skeletons had been found here. The sea lapped around my feet, on a pleasant early evening and I wondered what my mother would have made of my 'shoestring' enterprise? I think she would have been delighted and as supportive as ever of my racehorse adventures back in the old Country.

Me and Mum. Manchester September 1993.

GLOSSARY

For the uninitiated below are a list of terms used in the book, which you may find helpful.

Bay – Deep reddish brown coloured horse

Black Type – a horse that has won or been placed in a pattern/listed race, usually enhances their breeding value.

Broodmare – a mare kept for breeding

Bumper – national hunt flat race for prospective jumping horses

Chaser – a horse, which takes part in, jumps races over fences

Colours - The racing silks worn by jockeys, registered by the owner

Connections – owners and trainers of a horse.

Cut in the ground – the ground surface that has been softened by rain.

Dam – the mother of a horse.

Declared – a horse is confirmed to start in a race (usually 48 hours in advance for flat horses and 24 hours for jumps).

Favourite – the horse on which most money has been wagered

Frame – horses finishing in the first three places.

Furlong – one eighth of a mile or 220 yards and the distance in which races are measured.

Gelding – a male horse that has been castrated.

Going – official description of the racing surface, it is determined by the amount of moisture in the ground. This can range from heavy, soft, good and firm.

Graded races – the top tier of races. On the flat group 1 is the highest category, with group 2 and 3 in descending order. Over the jumps, the top tier is grade 1 with grade 2 and 3 in descending order.

Green – an inexperienced horse

Handicap – the BHA allocate a different weight for each horse to carry. After a horse has run usually three times it is allocated an official handicap mark that determines the weight it will carry in a handicap race.

HRI – Horse Racing Ireland

Hurdler – a horse that races over hurdles, which are lighter and lower than fences

Juvenile – two year old horse

Length – the unit of measurement for the winning margin, the measurement of a horse from head to tail

Listed race – a class of race just below group (flat) or graded (jumps).

Maiden – a horse that hasn't yet won a race.

Napped – best bet according to a tipster

Odds on – strong favourite, where winnings are less than the stake

Off the bridle – a tired horse reduces his effort

Outsider – Long priced horse in the betting, viewed as unlikely to win

Photo Finish – Electronic photo device that determines minimal distances in a close finish

Pulled up – a horse that drops out of the race, a non-finisher.

Rating – a measure of a horse's ability usually on a scale from 0 to over 100. There are different official rating figures for flat and national hunt horses.

Ring – parade ring where connections meet as horse parades.

Schooled – Practice whatever it is your training the horse to do.

Sire – father of a horse.

Stallion – an entire horse used for breeding purposes

Starting Price (SP) – Official odds of a horse at which bets are settled

String – all the horses in a particular training stable.

Thanks a Million – effusive thanks offered both on the racecourse and in the bar!

Timber – racing over hurdles

Under Starter's Orders – the time the runners are deemed to be ready to race

Winner Alright – Terminology used by the steward on Irish racecourses to confirm that the horse race result stands – unfortunately not heard for one of my horses during the course of this journey!

Yearling – a horse of either sex during 1 January to 31 December following the year of its birth.

Steve spent over thirty years teaching sixth form students and has enjoyed the fruits of early retirement by returning to writing. Despite the demands of the day job, Steve did find time to write two books on his first sporting passion football. One proved to be a best seller, satisfied with his efforts Steve laid down his pen.

Smitten by the racehorse ownership bug, he has recently concentrated his writing on this theme; this Irish odyssey is the final book in a trilogy on that topic.

He has moved from Mr Ed's initial equine influence, to taking up investments with the Jockey Club and in recent years 'owning' a whole series of racehorses. Despite the annual charms of the Cheltenham Festival he is happy living with his wife Sue in Manchester.

Printed in Great Britain
by Amazon

36701552R00056